TEACHER'S PET PUBLICATIONS

LITPLAN TEACHER PACK
for
To Kill a Mockingbird

based on the book by
Harper Lee

Written by
Mary B. Collins

© 1999 Teacher's Pet Publications
All Rights Reserved

This **LitPlan** for Harper Lee's
To Kill a Mockingbird
has been brought to you by Teacher's Pet Publications, Inc.

Copyright Teacher's Pet Publications 1999
11504 Hammock Point
Berlin MD 21811

Only the student materials in this unit plan may be reproduced. Pages such as worksheets and study guides may be reproduced for use in the purchaser's classroom. For any additional copyright questions, contact Teacher's Pet Publications.

TABLE OF CONTENTS - *To Kill A Mockingbird*

Introduction	5
Unit Objectives	8
Reading Assignment Sheet	9
Unit Outline	10
Study Questions (Short Answer)	13
Quiz/Study Questions (Multiple Choice)	25
Pre-reading Vocabulary Worksheets	41
Lesson One (Introductory Lesson)	59
Nonfiction Assignment Sheet	61
Oral Reading Evaluation Form	63
Writing Assignment 1	65
Writing Assignment 2	78
Writing Assignment 3	79
Writing Evaluation Form	68
Vocabulary Review Activities	69
Extra Writing Assignments/Discussion ?s	71
Unit Review Activities	81
Unit Tests	85
Unit Resource Materials	115
Vocabulary Resource Materials	129

A FEW NOTES ABOUT THE AUTHOR
HARPER LEE

LEE, HARPER. *To Kill a Mockingbird* is fiction, but it has at least a few similarities to Harper Lee's own life. Like her character Scout, Harper Lee attended public schools and her father was an attorney.

Harper Lee was born in Monroeville, Alabama on Arpil 28, 1926. After attending public schools, she studied law at the University of Alabama, but she never completed her law degree. She moved to New York where she worked as an airline reservation clerk and pursued her writing career.

In 1961 Miss Lee won the Pulitzer Prize for fiction for *To Kill a Mockingbird*.

INTRODUCTION

This unit has been designed to develop students' reading, writing, thinking, and language skills through exercises and activities related to *To Kill A Mockingbird* by Harper Lee. It includes eighteen lessons, supported by extra resource materials.

The **introductory lesson** introduces students to one main theme of the novel through a game-type activity. Following the introductory activity, students are given a transition to explain how the activity relates to the book they are about to read. Following the transition, students are given the materials they will be using during the unit. At the end of the lesson, students begin the pre-reading work for the first reading assignment.

The **reading assignments** are approximately thirty pages each; some are a little shorter while others are a little longer. Students have approximately 15 minutes of pre-reading work to do prior to each reading assignment. This pre-reading work involves reviewing the study questions for the assignment and doing some vocabulary work for 8 to 10 vocabulary words they will encounter in their reading.

The **study guide questions** are fact-based questions; students can find the answers to these questions right in the text. These questions come in two formats: short answer required or multiple choice. The best use of these materials is probably to use the short answer version of the questions as study guides for students (since answers will be more complete), and to use the multiple choice version for occasional quizzes. It might be a good idea to make transparencies of your answer keys for the overhead projector.

The **vocabulary work** is intended to enrich students' vocabularies as well as to aid in the students' understanding of the book. Prior to each reading assignment, students will complete a two-part worksheet for approximately 8 to 10 vocabulary words in the upcoming reading assignment. Part I focuses on students' use of general knowledge and contextual clues by giving the sentence in which the word appears in the text. Students are then to write down what they think the words mean based on the words' usage. Part II nails down the definitions of the words by giving students dictionary definitions of the words and having students match the words to the correct definitions based on the words' contextual usage. Students should then have a good understanding of the words when they meet them in the text.

After each reading assignment, students will go back and formulate answers for the study guide questions. Discussion of these questions serves as a **review** of the most important events and ideas presented in the reading assignments.

After students complete reading the work, there is a **vocabulary review** lesson which pulls together all of the fragmented vocabulary lists for the reading assignments and gives students a review of all of the words they have studied.

Following the vocabulary review, a lesson is devoted to the **extra discussion questions/writing assignments**. These questions focus on interpretation, critical analysis and personal response, employing a variety of thinking skills and adding to the students' understanding of the novel.

The **group activity** which follows the discussion questions has students working in small groups to discuss the main themes of the novel. Using the information they have acquired so far through individual work and class discussions, students get together to further examine the text and to brainstorm ideas relating to the themes of the novel.

The group activity is followed by a **reports and discussion** session in which the groups share their ideas about the themes with the entire class; thus, the entire class is exposed to information about all of the themes and the entire class can discuss each theme based on the nucleus of information brought forth by each of the groups.

There are three **writing assignments** in this unit, each with the purpose of informing, persuading, or having students express personal opinions. The first assignment is to inform: students write a letter from Dill to his mother telling her all about his new friend, Scout. The second assignment is to persuade: following the reports and discussion, students take a stance regarding one of the themes the class has discussed, based on the information given in class and the students' own personal reflections. The third assignment is to give students a chance to simply express their own opinions and be creative: students do a group writing assignment in which they either outline the plot for *To Kill a Mockingbird II*, or outline a plot for *To Kill A Mockingbird* set in a major city in the current year.

In addition, there is a **nonfiction reading assignment**. Students are required to read a piece of nonfiction related in some way to *To Kill A Mockingbird* (articles about prejudice or coming of age, trial transcripts, etc.). After reading their nonfiction pieces, students will fill out a worksheet on which they answer questions regarding facts, interpretation, criticism, and personal opinions. During one class period, students make **oral presentations** about the nonfiction pieces they have read. This not only exposes all students to a wealth of information, it also gives students the opportunity to practice **public speaking**.

The **review lesson** pulls together all of the aspects of the unit. The teacher is given four or five choices of activities or games to use which all serve the same basic function of reviewing all of the information presented in the unit.

The **unit test** comes in two formats: all multiple choice-matching-true/false or with a mixture of matching, short answer, multiple choice, and composition. As a convenience, two different tests for each format have been included.

There are additional **support materials** included with this unit. The **extra activities section** includes suggestions for an in-class library, crossword and word search puzzles related to the novel, and extra vocabulary worksheets. There is a list of **bulletin board ideas** which gives the teacher suggestions for bulletin boards to go along with this unit. In addition, there is a list of **extra class activities** the teacher could choose from to enhance the unit or as a substitution for an exercise the teacher might feel is inappropriate for his/her class. **Answer keys** are located directly after the **reproducible student materials** throughout the unit. The student materials may be reproduced for use in the teacher's classroom without infringement of copyrights. No other portion of this unit may be reproduced without the written consent of Teacher's Pet Publications, Inc.

The **level** of this unit can be varied depending upon the criteria on which the individual assignments are graded, the teacher's expectations of his/her students in class discussions, and the formats chosen for the study guides, quizzes and test. If teachers have other ideas/activities they wish to use, they can usually easily be inserted prior to the review lesson.

UNIT OBJECTIVES *To Kill A Mockingbird*

1. Through reading Lee's *To Kill A Mockingbird*, students will gain a better understanding of typically American views and conflicts regarding education, prejudice, bravery, and respect of the individual.

2. Students will demonstrate their understanding of the text on four levels: factual, interpretive, critical and personal.

3. Students will define their own viewpoints on the aforementioned themes.

4. Students will be exposed to a different era of American life, showing many of today's conflicts are not new; they are rooted in our American past.

5. Students will see that each of our daily life experiences changes us and shapes our thoughts and feelings.

6. Students will be given the opportunity to practice reading aloud and silently to improve their skills in each area.

7. Students will answer questions to demonstrate their knowledge and understanding of the main events and characters in *To Kill A Mockingbird* as they relate to the author's theme development.

8. Students will enrich their vocabularies and improve their understanding of the novel through the vocabulary lessons prepared for use in conjunction with the novel.

9. The writing assignments in this unit are geared to several purposes:
    a. To have students demonstrate their abilities to inform, to persuade, or to express their own personal ideas
        Note: Students will demonstrate ability to write effectively to <u>inform</u> by developing and organizing facts to convey information. Students will demonstrate the ability to write effectively to <u>persuade</u> by selecting and organizing relevant information, establishing an argumentative purpose, and by designing an appropriate strategy for an identified audience. Students will demonstrate the ability to write effectively to <u>express personal ideas</u> by selecting a form and its appropriate elements.
    b. To check the students' reading comprehension
    c. To make students think about the ideas presented by the novel
    d. To encourage logical thinking

READING ASSIGNMENT SHEET - *To Kill A Mockingbird*

Date Assigned	Reading Assignments (Chapters)	Completion Date
	1-3	
	4-7	
	8-9	
	10-11	
	12-14	
	15-17	
	18-21	
	22-25	
	26-31	

UNIT OUTLINE - *To Kill A Mockingbird*

1 Introduction PV 1-3	2 Read 1-3 Orally	3 Study ?s 1-3 PVR 4-7	4 Quiz 4-7 PVR 8-9	5 Writing Assignment 1 PVR 10-11
6 Study ?s 8-11 PVR 12-14	7 Study ?s 12-14 PVR 15-21	8 Working Session Writing Conf.	9 Study ?s 15-21 PVR 22-25 Assign PVR 26-31	10 Study ?s 22-31 Vocabulary
11 Discussion	12 Group Activity	13 Reports & Discussion	14 Writing Assignment 2	15 Nonfiction Discussion
16 Group Writing Assignment (3)	17 Review	18 Test		

Key: P = Preview Study Questions   V = Vocabulary Work   R = Read

STUDY GUIDE QUESTIONS

SHORT ANSWER STUDY GUIDE QUESTIONS - *To Kill A Mockingbird*

Chapters 1-3
1. Identify Atticus Finch, Jean Louise (Scout) Finch, Jem Finch, Maycomb, Calpurnia, Charles Baker (Dill) Harris, The Radley Place, Stephanie Crawford, Arthur (Boo) Radley, Miss Caroline Fisher, Walter Cunningham, and Burris Ewell.
2. What did Dill dare Jem to do?
3. What was Scout's first "crime" at school?
4. What was Calpurnia's fault?
5. Why did Scout rub Walter Cunningham's nose in the dirt?
6. Scout said, " He ain't company, Cal, he's just a Cunningham." What did she mean by that, and what was Cal's answer?
7. What two mistakes did Miss Caroline make on the first day of school?
8. Why didn't the Ewells have to go to school?

Chapters 4-7
1. What did Scout and Jem find in the Radleys' tree?
2. Identify Mrs. Dubose.
3. How did Jem get even with Scout for contradicting him about "Hot Steams?"
4. What was the Boo Radley game?
5. Identify Miss Maudie.
6. What does Miss Maudie think of the Radleys?
7. Why do Dill and Jem want to give Boo Radley a note? What does Atticus say when he finds out about their plan?
8. How did Jem lose his pants? What did he find when he went back for them?
9. What else did Jem and Scout find in the Radleys' tree?
10. Why would there be no more surprises in the tree?

Chapters 8-9
1. What happened to Miss Maudie's house? What was her reaction?
2. Identify Cecil Jacobs.
3. What "disaster" happened at Christmas between Scout and Francis?
4. What did Scout's Uncle Jack learn from Scout and Atticus?

Chapters 10-11
1. What brave thing does Atticus do in Chapter 10? Why are Scout and Jem shocked?
2. What did Jem do when Mrs. Dubose said Atticus "lawed for niggers?"
3. What was Jem's punishment?
4. What did Jem learn from his encounter with Mrs. Dubose and following her death?

Mockingbird Short Answer Study Questions Page 2

Chapters 12-14
1. How does Jem change?
2. Identify Lula, Zeebo and Reverend Sykes.
3. What does Scout learn about Calpurnia?
4. Who was waiting for the children when they came home from the church service? Why had she come?
5. "Aunt Alexandra fitted into the world of Maycomb like a hand in a glove, but never into the world of Jem and me." Explain.
6. Atticus and Alexandra disagree about how to deal with the children. How does Atticus handle the situation?
7. Describe Jem and Scout's relationship through these chapters as Jem matures.
8. Why did Dill run away from home back to Maycomb?

Chapters 15-17
1. What did Mr. Heck Tate's mob want?
2. What was the purpose of Walter Cunningham's mob?
3. Why did Mr. Cunningham's mob leave?
4. Identify Mr. Dolphus Raymond.
5. Identify Tom Robinson, Mr. Gilmer, Bob Ewell, Mayella Ewell, and Judge Taylor.
6. What was the importance of Mayella's bruises being primarily on the right-hand side of her face?

Chapters 18-21
1. What was Mayella's account of the incident with Tom Robinson?
2. What was Tom's side of the story?
3. What was Tom's handicap? Why was it important to his case?
4. What do Dill and Scout learn from Mr. Raymond?
5. What were Atticus' closing remarks to the jury?
6. What was the jury's verdict?

Chapters 22-25
1. Why did Jem cry?
2. What was "'round the back steps" when Calpurnia came in on Monday morning?
3. What was the significance of Maudie's two little cakes and one large one?
4. Describe Bob Ewell's meeting with Atticus at the post office.
5. What is Atticus' reaction to Ewell's threats?
6. Alexandra doesn't want Scout playing with Walter Cunningham. Why not?
7. Jem said. "I think I'm beginning to understand why Boo Radley's stayed shut up in the house all this time . . . it's because he wants to stay inside." Why does he say that?

Mockingbird Short Answer Study Questions Page 3

8. Mrs. Merriweather of the missionary circle complains about her cooks and field hands. What does that tell us about her?
9. What happened to Tom Robinson?
10. What more do we learn about Alexandra after Atticus and Calpurnia leave?
11. What did Mr. Underwood's editorial say?

Chapters 26-31

1. What was Scout's fantasy regarding Arthur (Boo) Radley?
2. What did Scout hear Miss Gates say at the courthouse? In class, Miss Gates said, "That's the difference between America and Germany. We are a democracy and Germany is a dictatorship. . . . We don't believe in persecuting anybody. Persecution comes from people who are prejudiced." What does this tell us about Miss Gates?
3. What happened to Judge Taylor?
4. What happened to Helen Robinson?
5. What was Scout's part in the pageant?
6. Why did Scout and Jem not leave the school until almost everyone else had gone?
7. What happened to Jem and Scout on the way home from the pageant?
8. Who saved Jem and Scout? Who killed Bob Ewell?
9. Why did Heck Tate insist that Bob Ewell fell on his own knife?
10. Scout arranged things so that "if Miss Stephanie Crawford was watching from her upstairs window, she would see Arthur Radley escorting [her] down the sidewalk, as any gentleman would do." Why did she do that?
11. As Scout leaves the Radley porch, she looks out at the neighborhood and recounts the events of the last few years from the Radleys' perspective. Why is that important?

STUDY GUIDE QUESTIONS - *To Kill A Mockingbird*
Short Answer Format Answer Key

Chapters 1-3

1. Identify Atticus Finch, Jean Louise (Scout) Finch, Jem Finch, Maycomb, Calpurnia, Charles Baker (Dill) Harris, The Radley Place, Stephanie Crawford, Arthur (Boo) Radley, Miss Caroline Fisher, Walter Cunningham, and Burris Ewell.

    Atticus Finch is a lawyer and Scout and Jem's father. Scout is the narrator of the story. Jem is Scout's older brother. Maycomb is the name of the town (and also the county) where the story takes place. Calpurnia is the Finch family's cook, maid and nanny. Dill is Miss Rachael's nephew, a young boy who visits his aunt and plays with Scout and Jem in the summertime. The Radley Place is the home of the Radley family across the street from Scout's house; it is a curiosity to the children because the Radleys are so different from other folks they know. Stephanie Crawford is a gossipy neighbor who knows everybody's business and everyone's family history. Boo Radley is a mystery to the children; he never leaves his house. Miss Caroline Fisher is Scout's first grade teacher. Walter Cunningham is a student in Scout's class, one of The Cunninghams. Burris Ewell is also a student in Scout's class; he is one of The Ewells.

2. What did Dill dare Jem to do?

    Dill dared Jem to run up and touch the Radley house.

3. What was Scout's first "crime" at school?

    Scout's first crime was that she could already read.

4. What was Calpurnia's fault?

    Scout said it was Calpurnia's fault that she could write. This also caused trouble for her at school. Miss Caroline asked Scout to tell her father to stop teaching her.

5. Why did Scout rub Walter Cunningham's nose in the dirt?

    Scout stood up for Walter in class and tried to explain the Cunningham ways to Miss Caroline. For her explanations, Scout got in more trouble with Miss Caroline, so she took out her revenge on Walter.

6. Scout said, " He ain't company, Cal, he's just a Cunningham." What did she mean by that and what was Cal's answer?

    Scout meant that Finches were better than Cunninghams, and for that reason she didn't have to treat Walter as company. Calpurnia told Scout that she should treat anyone who came to visit her home as "company" and show him every courtesy.

7. What two mistakes did Miss Caroline make on the first day of school?

    Miss Caroline's first mistake was to offer Walter Cunningham money; the Cunninghams don't take anything they can't pay back. Her second mistake was trying to tell Burris Ewell to go home and wash out his "cooties."

8. Why didn't the Ewells have to go to school?

If the truant officer enforced the laws for the Ewells, Mr. Ewell would probably be jailed. Without their father, wretched as he was, the children would be worse off than if they simply did not go to school. Because the Ewell children's home life was so unusual, the authorities bent the rules for them.

<u>Chapters 4-7</u>

1. What did Scout and Jem find in the Radleys' tree?

They found gum and two Indian head pennies.

2. Identify Mrs. Dubose.

Mrs. Dubose is an old lady who lives down the street. She berates the children as they walk past her house.

3. How did Jem get even with Scout for contradicting him about "Hot Steams?"

When it was her turn to ride in the tire, he gave her an extra-hard shove. She ended up in the Radleys' front yard.

4. What was the Boo Radley game?

Jem, Dill and Scout reenacted the few facts and many peculiar stories they had heard about the Radleys.

5. Identify Miss Maudie.

Miss Maudie is another neighbor, about the age of Atticus. She is open-minded and enjoys the children's company.

6. What does Miss Maudie think of the Radleys?

She thinks they have a right to do whatever they want to do as long as they are not bothering anyone else, and she believes they have a right to their privacy.

7. Why do Dill and Jem want to give Boo Radley a note? What does Atticus say when he finds out about their plan?

They want to invite him out to play with them; they think he might enjoy that. Atticus tells the boys to leave Arthur Radley alone, that if he wanted to be outside, he would. Atticus also tells them that the proper way to extend the invitation would be at the Radley front door instead of putting a note on a fishing pole and sticking that through the window.

8. How did Jem lose his pants? What did he find when he went back for them?

Jem, Scout and Dill went to look into the Radley house. When they were discovered, they ran. Jem got caught on the fence, and in an effort to free himself, he took off his pants and left them on the fence. When he went back for them, they were mended and folded, sitting on the fence.

9. What else did Jem and Scout find in the Radleys' tree?
   They found a ball of twine, two figures (resembling themselves) carved from soap, and a broken watch.

10. Why would there be no more surprises in the tree?
    Mr. Nathan Radley cemented the hole closed.

Chapters 8-9
1. What happened to Miss Maudie's house? What was her reaction?
   Miss Maudie left fires going (for warmth) and her house burned down. As always, she put her most optimistic foot forward and seemed not to mind too much.

2. Identify Cecil Jacobs.
   Cecil Jacobs was a boy at Scout's school who first made her aware that Atticus was defending a black man.

3. What "disaster" happened at Christmas between Scout and Francis?
   Scout and Francis got into a fight because Francis was fussing with Scout about Atticus' defending a black man. Scout couldn't stand all the things Francis was calling Atticus, so she hit him square in the mouth. She didn't really understand what Francis said, but she knew it wasn't complimentary.

4. What did Scout's Uncle Jack learn from Scout and Atticus?
   Uncle Jack broke up the fight between Scout and Francis. He automatically took Francis' side. Since Francis was injured, he looked like the wronged party. Scout just gave in to Uncle Jack and said she did what he said she did. Later, she points out to Jack that he didn't even give her a chance to explain, that Atticus always listens to both sides before he decides which person is guilty. Secondly, when Scout asks Uncle Jack a question, he gives her a non-answer. Atticus later explains to Jack that such answers only confuse kids. The truth is always best.

Chapters 10-11
1. What brave thing does Atticus do in Chapter 10? Why are Scout and Jem shocked?
   Atticus shoots a mad dog. They are shocked because until this day, they think of Atticus as having no real talents or anything to be proud of. He never touched a gun, to their knowledge, and he did not believe in fighting. Thus, they are very surprised to find out about "One-Shot Finch."

2. What did Jem do when Mrs. Dubose said Atticus "lawed for niggers?"
   He took Scout's birthday baton and, waving it madly, cut the tops off of all of Mrs. Dubose's camellia bushes.

3. What was Jem's punishment?

   He had to repair the damage as well as he could, and he had to read to Mrs. Dubose each afternoon after school for a month.

4. What did Jem learn from his encounter with Mrs. Dubose and following her death?

   He learned that people aren't always what they seem, that one can't understand someone else until one has all the facts, and, most importantly, that there is a different kind of courage than physical courage.

<u>Chapters 12-14</u>

1. How does Jem change?

   Jem is growing up. He is trying to make sense of things he sees, trying to be like Atticus, and trying to put behind him childish games and youthful pranks. Consequently, he is moody sometimes and occasionally seems to lord his authority over Scout. She resents his new "airs."

2. Identify Lula, Zeebo and Reverend Sykes.

   Lula was the woman at Calpurnia's church who made Scout and Jem feel unwelcome. Zeebo, Cal's son, makes them feel welcome, as does Reverend Sykes, the preacher at Calpurnia's church.

3. What does Scout learn about Calpurnia?

   Scout learns that Cal leads a double life. She talks and acts like her black friends and neighbors when she is with them, and she talks and acts more like white people when she is with them. Scout thinks this is interesting and asks to visit Cal at her home one day.

4. Who was waiting for the children when they came home from the church service? Why had she come?

   Aunt Alexandra was waiting for them. She had come to stay and "help out" while Atticus would be busy with the Robinson trial.

5. "Aunt Alexandra fitted into the world of Maycomb like a hand in a glove, but never into the world of Jem and me." Explain.

   Alexandra knew all the proper social things to say and do, and she knew a great deal of the history of the local families. She joined some clubs and entertained at her home, and generally did fit right into the town's society. However, Alexandra didn't understand or agree with the values by which Atticus was raising his children. Therefore, she did not understand the children's behavior. Because their value systems were different, they were more often than not at odds.

6. Atticus and Alexandra disagree about how to deal with the children. How does Atticus handle the situation?

   Atticus makes the children obey Alexandra, but he lets them know that their relationship with him will always be the same as it was. He tries to appease Alexandra when he can, but on the major issues, he puts his foot down.

7. Describe Jem and Scout's relationship through these chapters as Jem matures.

   Jem and Scout seem to grow apart, but they don't really. They fuss more often than they had, mostly because Scout resents Jem's telling her what to do. Actually, though, they are still very close and join forces when their pride is at stake.

8. Why did Dill run away from home back to Maycomb?

   Dill had everything a boy could want, except his parents didn't spend any time with him. He didn't feel like they needed him.

Chapters 15-17

1. What did Mr. Heck Tate's mob want?

   They wanted to make sure Atticus and Tom Robinson would be all right.

2. What was the purpose of Walter Cunningham's mob?

   Cunningham's mob wanted to get to Tom Robinson to inflict their own justice upon him. If that meant they had to beat up Atticus, they were willing to do that.

3. Why did Mr. Cunningham's mob leave?

   Scout, Jem and Dill arrived on the scene. Scout came forward, and, while making her entrance and looking at the crowd, she noticed Mr. Cunningham. She identified him and began speaking to him on a personal basis, saying she was in his son's class and that he had come to lunch. She also reminded him that Atticus had done some legal work for him. All of these things were said in an innocent conversation to Mr. Cunningham. It made Cunningham (and others, I suspect), realize that they were individuals, neighbors, and that they really didn't want to hurt Atticus or anyone else.

4. Identify Mr. Dolphus Raymond.

   Mr. Dolphus Raymond was a white man who married a black woman and lived with the black community. Jem has heard a story that Mr. Raymond is always drunk. (However, we learn later that this is just an act.)

5. Identify Tom Robinson, Mr. Gilmer, Bob Ewell, Mayella Ewell, and Judge Taylor.

   Tom Robinson supposedly raped Mayella Ewell, Bob Ewell's daughter. Mr. Gilmer is the prosecuting attorney. Judge Taylor will be the judge during Tom's trial.

6. What was the importance of Mayella's bruises being primarily on the right-hand side of her face?

    Bruises on her right side indicate that a left-handed person inflicted the wounds.

Chapters 18-21

1. What was Mayella's account of the incident with Tom Robinson?

    Mayella said she asked Tom to come into the yard to break up a chiffarobe. When she went into the house to get him a nickel, he had followed her in and then he grabbed her around the neck and hit her. He "chunked [her] on the floor an' choked [her] 'n took advantage of [her]." Her father came in and was standing over her, and then she fainted.

2. What was Tom's side of the story?

    Mayella asked Tom to come fix the hinges on the door in the house. Mayella had saved enough nickels to send all of the kids out for ice cream so she and Tom would be alone. She asked Tom to climb up on a chair to get a box, and as he stood there, she grabbed him around the legs. When he hopped down off the chair, she jumped on him. She kissed him on the side of the face. Tom wanted out and had to push Mayella away from the door. She was not hurt. He ran away before Mr. Ewell could catch him.

3. What was Tom's handicap? Why was it important to his case?

    Tom's left arm had been rendered useless in an accident. He could not have bruised Mayella's right side and he more than probably would not have physically been able to force himself on a strong, violently resisting young woman.

4. What do Dill and Scout learn from Mr. Raymond?

    Dill and Scout learn that people aren't always as they appear to be. They learn that Mr. Raymond lives as he does because that's simply what he wants to do. Since people could never accept that, he gives them a "reason to latch onto" so they can accept his behavior. (One might note that Boo Radley does as he pleases, but gives people no reason to latch onto, and people make up their own reasons, no matter how ridiculous.)

5. What were Atticus' closing remarks to the jury?

    He said there was no medical evidence to suggest that Mayella had been raped, that the only evidence was the questionable testimony of two witnesses. He painted a picture of Mayella as a victim of poverty and ignorance, a lonely young woman who tempted and kissed a Negro and then had to get rid of him, the evidence, of her crime against society's unspoken laws. He tried to remind the jury of Thomas Jefferson's words that "all men are created equal," and that their job as a jury was to give a fair trial to the defendant.

6. What was the jury's verdict?

    The jury found Tom Robinson guilty.

Chapters 22-25

1. Why did Jem cry?

    Jem cried because he was shocked at the injustice of the jury, people from his own town, which he had always considered above such prejudice.

2. What was " 'round the back steps" when Calpurnia came in on Monday morning?

    The black community had left all kinds of food for Atticus and his family as a gesture of their thanks for his defending Tom Robinson.

3. What was the significance of Maudie's two little cakes and one large one?

    Maudie had two little cakes for Scout and Dill, but Jem got a slice from the big cake. This was Maudie's symbolic way of saying she accepted Jem as a young man instead of a boy.

4. Describe Bob Ewell's meeting with Atticus at the post office.

    Bob Ewell wanted to fight with Atticus. Atticus just said he was too old to fight, and he walked away. Bob Ewell threatened to get even.

5. What is Atticus' reaction to Ewell's threats?

    He rationally understands that Ewell is upset, and he allows Mr. Ewell the right to be upset. However, he does not believe that Bob Ewell would actually do any terrible physical harm to anyone.

6. Alexandra doesn't want Scout playing with Walter Cunningham. Why not?

    Alexandra thinks the Cunninghams are trash because they don't have the "background" of the Finches.

7. Jem said, "I think I'm beginning to understand why Boo Radley's stayed shut up in the house all this time . . . it's because he wants to stay inside." Why does he say that?

    The world is starting to look mighty complicated to Jem. The jury decision, all the talk about social class and the problem of what exactly "background" means, and Mr. Raymond's false drinking problem are all weighing on his mind, and he's trying to get things all sorted out with nice, neat definitions. He is learning that things in the real world just aren't easy to sort-out and understand.

8. Mrs. Merriweather of the missionary circle complains about her cooks and field hands. What does that tell us about her?

    As a member of the missionary circle, she is very concerned about the personal welfare of many Africans, but in her own back yard, Mrs. Merriweather is as prejudiced as she can be.

9. What happened to Tom Robinson?

    Tom was shot when he tried to escape from prison.

10. What more do we learn about Alexandra after Atticus and Calpurnia leave?
　　Alexandra is given a more rounded personality in this section. We see clearly for the first time that she loves and is concerned for her brother. We see her take the news of Tom's death with great difficulty, yet she gathers herself together and carries on with her guests. She seems a bit more human and a bit more noble than she has been painted prior to this.

11. What did Mr. Underwood's editorial say?
　　He likened Tom's death to the senseless slaughter of songbirds by hunters and children.

Chapters 26-31

1. What was Scout's fantasy regarding Arthur (Boo) Radley?
　　She daydreamed that Boo would be sitting in the swing and they would chat as if they had chatted every day for all their lives. She wanted him to be "normal" like everyone else on the street.

2. What did Scout hear Miss Gates say at the courthouse? In class, Miss Gates said, "That's the difference between America and Germany. We are a democracy and Germany is a dictatorship. . . . We don't believe in persecuting anybody. Persecution comes from people who are prejudiced." What does this tell us about Miss Gates?
　　Scout heard Miss Gates at the courthouse saying that "it's time somebody taught 'em a lesson, they were gettin' way above themselves, an' the next thing they think they can do is marry us." Miss Gates is either a hypocrite or has not stopped to recognize that she is just as prejudiced as Hitler was, although for a different group of people.

3. What happened to Judge Taylor?
　　Someone (Bob Ewell, we assume) was breaking into the judge's house when the judge and his dog frightened him away.

4. What happened to Helen Robinson?
　　Helen Robinson walked the long way around to work to avoid the Ewell house because they "chunked at her" when she used the public road. Mr. Link Deas escorted Helen on the public road and threatened the Ewells. After that she had no trouble.

5. What was Scout's part in the pageant?
　　She was to be a ham. Her ham costume would later save her life.

6. Why did Scout and Jem not leave the school until almost everyone else had gone?
　　Scout was embarrassed because she fell asleep, came on stage late during the pageant and ruined Mrs. Merriweather's program.

7. What happened to Jem and Scout on the way home from the pageant?
　　Someone attacked them. Scout got tangled in her costume, someone knocked out Jem, there was a struggle and then Scout saw someone carrying Jem home.

8. Who saved Jem and Scout? Who killed Bob Ewell?
   Arthur (Boo) Radley saved Jem and Scout and he killed Bob Ewell.

9. Why did Heck Tate insist that Bob Ewell fell on his own knife?
   Heck figured out that Arthur had killed Bob Ewell, and he saw no sense in dragging the "hero" through a nasty, public ordeal. He thought it would be better to "let the dead bury the dead."

10. Scout arranged things so that "if Miss Stephanie Crawford was watching from her upstairs window, she would see Arthur Radley escorting [her] down the sidewalk, as any gentleman would do." Why did she do that?
    Scout now understands that Arthur Radley is a real person, not a freak. She wants him, in his public appearance, to look "normal" so that Miss Stephanie and (through Miss Stephanie's gossip) the rest of the town will begin to think of him as a real person, too.

11. As Scout leaves the Radley porch, she looks out at the neighborhood and recounts the events of the last few years from the Radleys' perspective. Why is that important?
    All through the book, she (and Jem and Dill) have been, at various times, taking Atticus' advice and putting themselves in someone else's shoes, looking at things from someone else's perspective. Each time they do this, they learn something new. It is appropriate that near the conclusion of the novel, Scout takes the most difficult stance of looking through the world from Arthur Radley's perspective.

MULTIPLE CHOICE STUDY GUIDE/QUIZ QUESTIONS - *To Kill A Mockingbird*

<u>Chapters 1-3</u>
I. Matching
- ___ 1. Jem
- ___ 2. Radley Place
- ___ 3. Boo
- ___ 4. Maycomb
- ___ 5. Walter
- ___ 6. Atticus
- ___ 7. Scout
- ___ 8. S. Crawford
- ___ 9. Burris
- ___ 10. Dill
- ___ 11. Calpurnia
- ___ 12. Miss Fisher

A. Miss Rachael's nephew who visits in the summer
B. Gossipy neighbor
C. A lawyer; Scout's father
D. Scout's brother
E. One of The Ewells
F. Boo's home
G. Narrator of the story
H. Finch family cook, maid & nanny
I. Setting
J. He never leaves his house
K. Scout's teacher
L. One of The Cunninghams

II. Multiple Choice

1. What did Dill dare Jem to do?
    a. Eat a goldfish
    b. Touch the Radley house
    c. Beat up Burris
    d. Sneak out at night

2. What was Scout's first "crime" at school?
    a. Could already read
    b. Sat next to a Ewell
    c. Was late
    d. Hit Walter

3. What was Calpurnia's fault?
    a. That Boo never left home
    b. Scout was late
    c. Scout could read
    d. Jem got sick

4. What did Scout do to Walter Cunningham?
    a. Threw a book at him
    b. Hid his books
    c. Rubbed his nose in dirt
    d. Ignored him

Mockingbird Study/Quiz Questions Multiple Choice Page 2

5. "He ain't company, Cal, he's just a Cunningham." What was Cal's response?
    a. She agreed.
    b. "Anyone who visits is company."
    c. She sent Scout to her room.
    d. She laughed.

6. What was one of Miss Caroline's mistakes on the first day of school?
    a. Arrived late
    b. Argued with Jem
    c. Offered Walter money
    d. Yelled at Scout

7. Why didn't the Ewells have to go to school?
    a. They were too poor.
    b. They had cooties.
    c. They lived too far away
    d. The authorities bent the rules for them because of their home life.

Mockingbird Study/Quiz Questions Multiple Choice Page 3

Chapters 4-7

1. What did Scout and Jem find in the Radleys' tree?
    a. Gum and pennies
    b. Books
    c. A dead bird
    d. A snake skin

2. What does Mrs. Dubose do to the children who walk past her house?
    a. Smiles & waves to them
    b. Peeps at them from behind her curtains
    c. Berates them
    d. Warns them about her dog

3. How did Jem get even with Scout for contradicting him about "Hot Steams?"
    a. Told Atticus
    b. Framed her for a trick on Cal
    c. Pushed her into the Radley yard
    d. Took her homework

4. What was the Boo Radley game?
    a. Running up to the Radley house and touching it
    b. Leaving trinkets in a tree
    c. Scaring each other
    d. Reenacting Boo Radley stories

5. Who is Miss Maudie?
    a. A good neighbor who likes the children
    b. Jem's teacher who lives next door
    c. Cal's sister
    d. Atticus' sister

6. What does Miss Maudie think of the Radleys?
    a. They should all be locked away.
    b. They all need a bath.
    c. She is afraid of them.
    d. They have a right to their privacy.

Mockingbird Study/Quiz Questions Multiple Choice Page 4

7. Why do Dill and Jem want to give Boo Radley a note?
    a. To invite him out to play
    b. To torment him
    c. To warn him
    d. To scare him

8. How did Jem lose his pants?
    a. Boo Radley stole them.
    b. He took them off to free himself from the fence.
    c. Scout played a trick on him.
    d. Miss Maudie took them to mend without telling him.

9. What else did Jem and Scout find in the Radleys' tree?
    a. Apples
    b. Jem's pants
    c. Twine, two figures & a watch
    d. Nothing

10. Why would there be no more surprises in the tree?
    a. Boo died.
    b. Atticus told them not to go there anymore.
    c. Birds were nesting there.
    d. Mr. Nathan Radley cemented the hole closed.

Mockingbird Study/Quiz Questions Multiple Choice Page 5

Chapters 8-11 True or False?

___ 1. Miss Maudie left fires going (for warmth) and her house burned down. As always, she put her most optimistic foot forward and seemed not to mind too much.

___ 2. Cecil Jacobs was a boy at Scout's school who made fun of Cal.

___ 3. Scout agreed with Francis' attitude towards Atticus' case.

___ 4. Uncle Jack treats the children just like Atticus does.

___ 5. Atticus shoots a mad dog, and the children are very surprised to find out about "One-Shot Finch."

___ 6. Jem cut the tops off of all of Mrs. Dubose's camellia bushes.

___ 7. Jem had to read to Miss Maudie each afternoon after school for a month.

___ 8. Jem learned that people aren't always what they seem, that one can't understand someone else until one has all the facts, and, most importantly, that there is a different kind of courage than physical courage.

Mockingbird Study/Quiz Questions Multiple Choice Page 6

Chapters 12-14
1. How does Jem change?
 a. He is moody sometimes.
 b. He "lords" his authority over Scout
 c. He is losing interest in childish games.
 d. All of the above

2. Who makes Scout and Jem feel welcome at Calpurnia's church?
 a. Zeebo
 b. Reverend Sykes
 c. Zeebo and Rev. Sykes
 d. Lula

3. What does Scout learn about Calpurnia?
 a. She is very ill.
 b. She leads a double life.
 c. She doesn't really like church.
 d. She has no family.

4. Who was waiting for the children when they came home from the church service?
 a. Mrs. Dubose
 b. Mrs. Robinson
 c. Uncle Jack
 d. Aunt Alexandra

5. Describe the relationship between Aunt Alexandra and the children.
 a. They were good friends.
 b. Alexandra was like their teacher.
 c. They were usually at odds with each other.
 d. Alexandra was just like Atticus to them.

6. Atticus and Alexandra disagree about how to deal with the children. How does Atticus handle the situation?
 a. He tries to appease Alexandra when he can, but on the major issues, he puts his foot down.
 b. He tells the children to do as they please.
 c. He tells Alexandra she must get his permission before correcting the children.
 d. He tells the children he trusts Alexandra's judgement and to follow all her instructions.

Mockingbird Study/Quiz Questions Multiple Choice Page 7

7. Describe Jem and Scout's relationship through these chapters as Jem matures.
    a. Jem and Scout seem to grow apart, but they don't really.
    b. They fuss more often than they had.
    c. They are actually still very close and join forces when their pride is at stake.
    d. All of the above

8. Why did Dill run away from home back to Maycomb?
    a. He hated his foster home.
    b. He didn't feel like his parents needed him.
    c. He secretly knew he should testify on behalf of Mr. Robinson.
    d. Boo needed him.

Mockingbird Study/Quiz Questions Multiple Choice Page 8

Chapters 15-17
I. Matching

___ 1. Dolphus Raymond   A. Was accused of raping Mayella

___ 2. Tom Robinson   B. The prosecuting attorney

___ 3. Bob Ewell   C. White man who lived in the black community

___ 4. Taylor   D. Mayella's father

___ 5. Mr. Gilmer   E. Judge

II. True or False

___ 6. Heck Tate's mob wanted to get Tom Robinson and inflict their own justice on him.

___ 7. Scout saved Atticus and Mr. Robinson from the mob.

___ 8. The bruises on Mayella's right side indicated that Tom Robinson was guilty.

Mockingbird Study/Quiz Questions Multiple Choice Page 9

Chapters 18-21

1. What was Mayella's account of the incident with Tom Robinson?
    a. When she went in the house to get him a nickel for chopping wood, he attacked her.
    b. When he was done chopping wood, he threatened her with the axe.
    c. He made all the kids go away and then attacked her.
    d. None of the above

2. What was Tom's side of the story?
    a. Absolutely nothing happened. He chopped wood and then went home.
    b. She lured him into the house and kissed him. He left immediately.
    c. She paid him to kiss her.
    d. None of the above

3. What was Tom's handicap?
    a. Blind in one eye
    b. Broken leg
    c. Broken right arm
    d. Left arm rendered useless

4. What do Dill and Scout learn from Mr. Raymond?
    a. Crime doesn't pay.
    b. People aren't always as they appear to be.
    c. Mobs don't solve anything.
    d. Some people never learn.

5. What were Atticus' closing remarks to the jury?
    a. There was no medical evidence to suggest that Mayella had been raped.
    b. The only evidence was the questionable testimony of two witnesses.
    c. Mayella was lonely and a victim of poverty and ignorance.
    d. All of the above

6. What was the jury's verdict?
    a. Guilty
    b. Not guilty
    c. Hung jury
    d. Mistrial

Mockingbird Study/Quiz Questions Multiple Choice Page 10

Chapters 22-25

1. Why did Jem cry?
    a. Tom was his best friend.
    b. Aunt Alexandra was leaving.
    c. He was shocked at the injustice of the jury.
    d. People were making fun of Atticus.

2. What was " 'round the back steps" when Calpurnia came in on Monday morning?
    a. Food
    b. A black cat
    c. A mob
    d. Boo Radley

3. What was the significance of Maudie's two little cakes and one large one?
    a. Dill and Scout had earned cakes of their own.
    b. Maudie just didn't have enough little cakes.
    c. The big piece was Scout's reward.
    d. Jem was no longer a kid.

4. Describe Bob Ewell's meeting with Atticus at the post office.
    a. They were friendly.
    b. Bob Ewell threatened Atticus.
    c. Atticus bragged about the court case.
    d. They had a fist fight.

5. What was Atticus' reaction to Ewell's threats?
    a. He understood Mr. Ewell's anger.
    b. He was insulted.
    c. He got mad.
    d. He filed a law suit.

6. Alexandra doesn't want Scout playing with Walter Cunningham. Why not?
    a. Walter is a bad boy.
    b. Cunninghams are not social equals of the Finches.
    c. She is afraid of him.
    d. Scout has been grounded.

Mockingbird Study/Quiz Questions Multiple Choice Page 11

7. Why does Jem think Boo stays inside?
    a. He is crazy.
    b. He is forced to against his will.
    c. Medical reasons
    d. The outside world is too complicated.

8. What word best describes Mrs. Merriweather?
    a. Brave
    b. Saintly
    c. Prejudiced
    d. Poor

9. What happened to Tom Robinson?
    a. A mob broke into the jail and killed him.
    b. Other prisoners killed him.
    c. Tom was shot when he tried to escape from prison.
    d. He was sent to a work camp and never heard from again.

10. What more do we learn about Alexandra after Atticus and Calpurnia leave?
    a. She is more noble and nicer than she appeared to be at first.
    b. She is really a witch.
    c. She came to run away from trouble, not just to help Atticus.
    d. She hates children.

11. Mr. Underwood's editorial likened Tom's death to the senseless slaying of ----.
    a. Cattle
    b. Songbirds
    c. Pigs
    d. Elephants

Mockingbird Study/Quiz Questions Multiple Choice Page 12

<u>Chapters 26-31</u>

1. What was Scout's fantasy regarding Arthur (Boo) Radley?
    a. Boo would run away with Tom Robinson, and they would both be safe.
    b. Boo would be lynched by a mob.
    c. She would rescue Boo.
    d. Boo would be normal.

2. What word best describes Mrs. Gates?
    a. Hypocrite
    b. Evil
    c. Stupid
    d. Ignorant

3. What happened to Judge Taylor?
    a. Someone ambushed him.
    b. He had an accident.
    c. Someone tried to break into his house.
    d. His wife died.

4. What happened to Helen Robinson?
    a. She was banished from the community.
    b. The Ewells "chunked" at her when she walked past their house on the main road.
    c. A mob killed her.
    d. She was robbed.

5. What was Scout's part in the pageant?
    a. An angel
    b. A vegetable
    c. A princess
    d. A ham

6. Why did Scout and Jem not leave the school until almost everyone else had gone?
    a. Scout was embarrassed.
    b. Jem fell asleep.
    c. It was Scout's punishment for messing up the play.
    d. They were waiting for Atticus.

Mockingbird Study/Quiz Questions Multiple Choice Page 13

7. What happened to Jem and Scout on the way home from the pageant?
    a. They got lost.
    b. Someone attacked them.
    c. They got run over.
    d. They were kidnaped.

8. Who killed Bob Ewell?
    a. Boo Radley
    b. The sheriff
    c. He killed himself.
    d. Atticus

9. Why did Heck Tate insist that Bob Ewell fell on his own knife?
    a. To cover up for himself
    b. To cover up for Boo
    c. To cover up for Tom Robinson
    d. Because he did

10. Scout arranged things so that "if Miss Stephanie Crawford was watching from her upstairs window, she would see Arthur Radley escorting [her] down the sidewalk, as any gentleman would do." Why did she do that?
    a. To make Miss Crawford jealous
    b. For protection
    c. To show off
    d. To show Miss Crawford that Boo is normal

11. At the end of the novel Scout looks at the world through who's perspective?
    a. Arthur Radley
    b. Atticus
    c. Jem
    d. Dill

ANSWER KEY - MULTIPLE CHOICE STUDY/QUIZ QUESTIONS
To Kill A Mockingbird

Chapters 1-3

I. Matching	II. Multiple Choice
1. D	1. B
2. F	2. A
3. J	3. C
4. I	4. C
5. L	5. B
6. C	6. C
7. G	7. D
8. B	
9. E	
10. A	
11. H	
12. K	

Chapters 4-7
1. A
2. C
3. C
4. D
5. A
6. D
7. A
8. B
9. C
10. D

Chapters 8-11
1. T
2. F
3. F
4. F
5. T
6. T
7. F
8. T

Chapters 12-14
1. D
2. C
3. B
4. D
5. C
6. C
7. D
8. B

Chapters 15-17
1. C
2. A
3. D
4. E
5. B
6. F
7. T
8. F

Chapters 18-21
1. A
2. B
3. D
4. B
5. D
6. A

Chapters 22-25
1. C
2. A
3. D
4. B
5. A
6. B
7. D
8. C
9. C
10. A
11. B

Chapters 26-31
1. D
2. A
3. C
4. B
5. D
6. A
7. B
8. A
9. B
10. D
11. A

PREREADING VOCABULARY WORKSHEETS

VOCABULARY - *To Kill A Mockingbird*

<u>Chapters 1-3</u> Part I: Using Prior Knowledge and Contextual Clues

Below are the sentences in which the vocabulary words appear in the text. Read the sentence. Use any clues you can find in the sentence combined with your prior knowledge, and write what you think the underlined words mean in the space provided.

1. Thus we came to know Dill as a pocket Merlin, whose head teemed with <u>eccentric</u> plans, strange longings, and quaint fancies.

2. Inside the house lived a <u>malevolent</u> phantom.

3. Nobody knew what form of <u>intimidation</u> Mr. Radley employed to keep Boo out of sight, but Jem figured that Mr. Radley kept him chained to the bed most of the time.

4. Jem <u>condescended</u> to take me to school the first day, a job usually done by one's parents, but Atticus had said Jem would be delighted to show me where my room was.

5. The class murmured apprehensively, should she prove to harbor her share of the peculiarities <u>indigenous</u> to that region.

6. Having never questioned Jem's <u>pronouncements,</u> I saw no reason to begin now.

7. Jem's free dispensation of my pledge <u>irked</u> me, but precious noontime minutes were ticking away.

8. Apparently she had revived enough to <u>persevere</u> in her profession.

9. "Do you know what a <u>compromise</u> is?" he asked.

Mockingbird Vocabulary - Chapters 1-3 Continued

Part II: Determining the Meaning

Match the vocabulary words to their dictionary definitions. If there are words for which you cannot figure out the definition by contextual clues and by process of elimination, look them up in a dictionary.

___ 1. eccentric
___ 2. malevolent
___ 3. intimidation
___ 4. condescended
___ 5. indigenous
___ 6. pronouncements
___ 7. irked
___ 8. persevere
___ 9. compromise

A. threats
B. authoritative statements
C. departing from the established norm, model, or rule
D. exhibiting or having ill-will; malicious
E. native
F. settlement of differences in which concessions are made
G. remain constant to a purpose in spite of obstacles
H. annoyed; bothered
I. to come down voluntarily to the level of inferiors

Vocabulary - *To Kill A Mockingbird* Chapters 4-7

Part I: Using Prior Knowledge and Contextual Clues

Below are the sentences in which the vocabulary words appear in the text. Read the sentence. Use any clues you can find in the sentence combined with your prior knowledge, and write what you think the underlined words mean on the lines provided.

1. For some reason, my first year of school had wrought a great change in our relationship: Calpurnia's tyranny, unfairness, and meddling in my business had faded to gentle grumblings of general disapproval.

2. Mrs. Dubose lived two doors up the street from us; neighborhood opinion was unanimous that Mrs. Dubose was the meanest old woman who ever lived.

3. Jem's evasion told me our game was a secret, so I kept quiet.

4. She was a widow, a chameleon lady who worked in her flower beds in an old straw hat and men's coveralls, but after her five o'clock bath she would appear on the porch and reign over the street in magisterial beauty.

5. "Son," he said to Jem, "I'm going to tell you something and tell you one time: stop tormenting that man. That goes for the other two of you."

6. Jem decided there was no point in quibbling, and was silent.

7. Jem skipped two steps, put his foot on the porch, heaved himself to it, and teetered a long moment.

8. Every night-sound I heard from my cot on the back porch was magnified three-fold; every scratch of feet on gravel was Boo Radley seeking revenge, every passing Negro laughing in the night was Boo Radley loose and after us; insects splashing against the screen were Boo Radley's insane fingers picking the wire to pieces; the chinaberry trees were malignant, hovering, alive.

Mockingbird Vocabulary - Chapters 4-7 Continued

Part II: Determining the Meaning
　　Match the vocabulary words to their dictionary definitions. If there are words for which you cannot figure out the definition by contextual clues and by process of elimination, look them up in a dictionary.

___ 10. tyranny
___ 11. unanimous
___ 12. evasion
___ 13. chameleon
___ 14. tormenting
___ 15. quibbling
___ 16. teetered
___ 17. malignant

A. moved unsurely in a see-sawing motion
B. like a lizard known for changing colors to match its surroundings; changeable person
C. making petty distinctions or irrelevant observations
D. actively evil in nature
E. in complete agreement
F. pestering; harassing
G. act of avoiding
H. extreme harshness or severity; rigor

Vocabulary - *To Kill A Mockingbird* Chapters 8-9

Part I: Using Prior Knowledge and Contextual Clues

    Below are the sentences in which the vocabulary words appear in the text. Read the sentence. Use any clues you can find in the sentence combined with your prior knowledge, and write what you think the underlined words mean on the lines provided.

1. She was <u>entrusted</u> with issuing public announcements, wedding invitations, setting off the fire siren, and giving first-aid instructions when Dr. Reynolds was away.

2. Roaring, the house collapsed; fire gushed everywhere, followed by a flurry of blankets from men on top of the <u>adjacent</u> houses, beating out sparks and burning chunks of wood.

3. She must have seen my <u>perplexity</u>.

4. He was a year older than I, and I avoided him on principle: he enjoyed everything I disapproved of, and disliked my <u>ingenuous</u> diversions.

5. Aunt Alexandra was <u>fanatical</u> on the subject of my attire.

6. Aunty had continued to <u>isolate</u> me long after Jem and Francis graduated to the big table.

7. I was <u>debating</u> whether to stand there or run, and tarried in indecision a moment too long: I turned to flee but Uncle Jack was quicker.

8. "The jury couldn't possibly be expected to take Tom Robinson's word against the Ewells' -- are you <u>acquainted</u> with the Ewells?"

Mockingbird Vocabulary - Chapters 8-9 Continued

Part II: Determining the Meaning

Match the vocabulary words to their dictionary definitions. If there are words for which you cannot figure out the definition by contextual clues and by process of elimination, look them up in a dictionary.

___ 21. entrusted
___ 22. adjacent
___ 23. perplexity
___ 24. ingenuous
___ 25. fanatical
___ 26. isolate
___ 27. debating
___ 28. acquainted

A. next to
B. without sophistication; artless; innocent
C. made familiar with
D. given over to another for care or protection
E. to separate from the group; set apart
F. the condition of being puzzled
G. possessed or driven by excessive zeal
H. deliberating; considering

Vocabulary - *To Kill A Mockingbird* Chapters 10-11

Part I: Using Prior Knowledge and Contextual Clues
   Below are the sentences in which the vocabulary words appear in the text. Read the sentence. Use any clues you can find in the sentence combined with your prior knowledge, and write what you think the underlined words mean on the lines provided.

1. He was much older than the parents of our school <u>contemporaries</u>, and there was nothing Jem or I could say about him when our classmates said, "My father--"

2. With these attributes, however, he would not remain as <u>inconspicuous</u> as we wished him to: that year, the school buzzed with talk about him defending Tom Robinson, none of which was complimentary.

3. "You're in considerable <u>peril</u>."

4. "Don't you <u>contradict</u> me!" Mrs. Dubose bawled.

5. Jem's lips moved, but his "Yes sir," was <u>inaudible</u>.

6. "She was conscious to the last, almost. Conscious," he smiled, " and <u>cantankerous</u>."

Part II: Determining the Meaning
   Match the vocabulary words to their dictionary definitions. If there are words for which you cannot figure out the definition by contextual clues and by process of elimination, look them up in a dictionary.

___ 29. contemporaries   A. unable to be heard
___ 30. inconspicuous   B. not readily noticeable
___ 31. peril   C. contrary; disagreeable; quarrelsome
___ 32. contradict   D. to go against
___ 33. inaudible   E. of the same time or era; about the same age
___ 34. cantankerous   F. danger

Vocabulary - *To Kill A Mockingbird* Chapters 12-14

Part I: Using Prior Knowledge and Contextual Clues
   Below are the sentences in which the vocabulary words appear in the text. Read the sentence. Use any clues you can find in the sentence combined with your prior knowledge, and write what you think the underlined words mean on the lines provided.

1. The fact that I had a fiance was little compensation for his absence: ...

2. I had never thought about it, but summer was Dill by the fishpool smoking string, Dill's eyes alive with complicated plans to make Boo Radley emerge, ...

3. In addition to Jem's newly developed characteristics, he had acquired a maddening air of wisdom.

4. There was no sign of piano, organ, hymn-books, church programs--the familiar ecclesiastical impedimenta we saw every Sunday.

5. There was a story behind all this, but I had no desire to extract it from her then: ...

6. I never understood her preoccupation with heredity.

7. Atticus looked pensive.

8. "Scout, try not to antagonize Aunty, hear?"

9. He traveled with the show all over Mississippi until his infallible sense of direction told him he was in Abbott County, Alabama, just across the river from Maycomb.

Mockingbird Vocabulary - Chapters 12-14 Continued

Part II: Determining the Meaning
　　Match the vocabulary words to their dictionary definitions. If there are words for which you cannot figure out the definition by contextual clues and by process of elimination, look them up in a dictionary.

___ 35. compensation　　　　A. to come forth from something
___ 36. emerge　　　　　　　B. to forcibly draw forth; pull out
___ 37. acquired　　　　　　 C. something given or received as substitution or payment
___ 38. ecclesiastical　　　　D. thoughtful
___ 39. extract　　　　　　　E. incur the dislike of someone; counteract
___ 40. preoccupation　　　　F. pertaining to a church
___ 41. pensive　　　　　　　G. unfailing; always correct
___ 42. antagonize　　　　　 H. obtained
___ 43. infallible　　　　　　I. the absorption of the attention or intellect

Vocabulary - *To Kill A Mockingbird* Chapters 15-17

Part I: Using Prior Knowledge and Contextual Clues

Below are the sentences in which the vocabulary words appear in the text. Use any clues you can find in the sentence combined with your prior knowledge, and write what you think the underlined words mean.

1. After many telephone calls, much pleading on behalf of the <u>defendant</u>, and a long forgiving letter from his mother, it was decided that Dill could stay.

2. I don't think anybody in Maycomb'll <u>begrudge</u> me a client, with times this hard.

3. He was sitting in one of his office chairs, and he was reading, <u>oblivious</u> of the nightbugs dancing over his head.

4. We were accustomed to prompt, if not always cheerful <u>acquiescence</u> to Atticus's instructions, but from the way he stood Jem was not thinking of budging.

5. Dill was <u>encumbered</u> by the chair, and his pace was slower.

6. ... he gave the impression of dozing, an impression <u>dispelled</u> forever when a lawyer once deliberately pushed a pile of books to the floor in a desperate effort to wake him up."

7. He permitted smoking in his courtroom but did not himself <u>indulge</u>: ...

8. Atticus was proceeding <u>amiably</u>, as if he were involved in a title dispute.

9. Mr. Ewell wrote on the back of the envelope and looked up <u>complacently</u> to see Judge Taylor staring at him as if her were some fragrant gardenia in full bloom on the witness stand ...

Mockingbird Vocabulary - Chapters 15-17 Continued

Part II: Determining the Meaning
　　Match the vocabulary words to their dictionary definitions. If there are words for which you cannot figure out the definition by contextual clues and by process of elimination, look them up in a dictionary.

___ 44. defendant　　　　　A. good-naturedly; cordially
___ 45. begrudge　　　　　B. person against whom an action is brought
___ 46. oblivious　　　　　C. done away with
___ 47. acquiescence　　　D. passive agreement
___ 48. encumbered　　　　E. to envy the possession or enjoyment of
___ 49. dispelled　　　　　F. in a self-satisfied manner
___ 50. indulge　　　　　　G. unaware
___ 51. amiably　　　　　　H. hindered
___ 52. complacently　　　I. to allow oneself a special pleasure

Vocabulary - *To Kill A Mockingbird* Chapters 18-21

Part I: Using Prior Knowledge and Contextual Clues

Below are the sentences in which the vocabulary words appear in the text. Read the sentence. Use any clues you can find in the sentence combined with your prior knowledge, and write what you think the underlined words mean on the lines provided.

1. ... there was something stealthy about hers, like a steady-eyed cat with a twitchy tail.

2. "State will not prejudice the witness against counsel for the defense ..."

3. Slowly but surely I began to see the pattern of Atticus's questions: from questions that Mr. Gilmer did not deem sufficiently irrelevant or immaterial to object to, Atticus was quietly building up before the jury a picture of the Ewell's home life.

4. Until my father explained it to me later, I did not understand the subtlety of Tom's predicament: he would not have dared strike a white woman under any circumstances and expect to live long, so he took the first opportunity to run--a sure sign of guilt.

5. I had never encountered a being who deliberately perpetrated fraud against himself.

6. She persisted, and her subsequent reaction is something that all of us have known at one time or another.

7. ... there is one human institution that makes a pauper the equal of a Rockefeller, the stupid man the equal of an Einstein, and the ignorant man the equal of any college president.

Mockingbird Vocabulary - Chapters 18-21 Continued
Part II: Determining the Meaning
    Match the vocabulary words to their dictionary definitions. If there are words for which you cannot figure out the definition by contextual clues and by process of elimination, look them up in a dictionary.

___ 53. stealthy   A. not applicable; having nothing to do with the matter at hand

___ 54. prejudice   B. something not obvious

___ 55. irrelevant   C. characterized by secret movement; avoiding notice

___ 56. subtlety   D. poor person

___ 57. predicament   E. troublesome situation

___ 58. fraud   F. preconceived preference or idea; bias

___ 59. subsequent   G. coming after

___ 60. pauper   H. deliberate deception for unfair or unlawful gain

Vocabulary - *To Kill A Mockingbird* Chapters 22-25

Part I: Using Prior Knowledge and Contextual Clues
   Below are the sentences in which the vocabulary words appear in the text. Read the sentence. Use any clues you can find in the sentence combined with your prior knowledge, and write what you think the underlined words mean on the lines provided.

1. Mr. Ewell was a veteran of an <u>obscure</u> war.

2. But when he noticed us dragging around the neighborhood, not eating, taking little interest in our normal <u>pursuits</u>, Atticus discovered how deeply frightened we were.

3. There is always the possibility, no matter how <u>improbable</u>, that he's innocent.

4. That jury took a few hours. An <u>inevitable</u> verdict, maybe, but usually it takes 'em just a few minutes.

5. Ladies in bunches always filled me with vague <u>apprehension</u> and a firm desire to be elsewhere

6. The last note would linger as long as there was air to <u>sustain</u> it.

7. Hypocrites, Mrs. Perkins, born <u>hypocrites</u>.

Part II: Determining the Meaning
   Match the vocabulary words to their dictionary definitions. If there are words for which you cannot figure out the definition by contextual clues and by process of elimination, look them up in a dictionary.

___ 61. obscure   A. people who say they believe one thing but actually believe
                             in the opposite
___ 62. pursuits   B. fearful feeling; dread
___ 63. improbable   C. activities; hobbies
___ 64. inevitable   D. not likely
___ 65. apprehension   E. inconspicuous; undistinguished; not well-known
___ 66. sustain   F. unavoidable; bound to happen
___ 67. hypocrites   G. to keep in existence; maintain; prolong

Vocabulary - *To Kill A Mockingbird* Chapters 26-31

Part I: Using Prior Knowledge and Contextual Clues
    Below are the sentences in which the vocabulary words appear in the text. Read the sentence. Use any clues you can find in the sentence combined with your prior knowledge, and write what you think the underlined words mean on the lines provided.

1. This practice <u>allegedly</u> overcame a variety of evils: ...

2. ... you'll learn that the Jews have been <u>persecuted</u> since the beginning of history, even driven out of their own country.

3. "I don't like it, Atticus, I don't like it at all," was Aunt Alexandra's <u>assessment</u> of these events.

4. ... --not even Jem could make me go through that crowd, and he <u>consented</u> to wait backstage with me until the audience left.

5. ... Jem knew as well as I that it was difficult to walk fast without stumping a toe, tripping on stones, and other <u>inconveniences</u>, and I was barefooted.

Part II: Determining the Meaning
    Match the vocabulary words to their dictionary definitions. If there are words for which you cannot figure out the definition by contextual clues and by process of elimination, look them up in a dictionary.

___ 68. allegedly   A. agreed to
___ 69. persecuted   B. supposedly; believed to be so but not yet proved
___ 70. assessment   C. things that cause trouble, lack of ease, or difficulty
___ 71. consented   D. evaluation
___ 72. inconveniences   E. oppressed; ill-treated

ANSWER KEY - VOCABULARY
To Kill A Mockingbird

Chapters 1-3	Chapters 4-7	Chapters 8-9	Chapters 10-11
1. C	10. H	21. D	29. E
2. D	11. E	22. A	30. B
3. A	12. G	23. F	31. F
4. I	13. B	24. B	32. D
5. E	14. F	25. G	33. A
6. B	15. C	26. E	34. C
7. H	16. A	27. H	
8. G	17. D	28. C	
9. F			

Chapters 12-14	Chapters 15-17	Chapters 18-21	Chapters 22-25
35. C	44. B	53. C	61. E
36. A	45. E	54. F	62. C
37. H	46. G	55. A	63. D
38. F	47. D	56. B	64. F
39. B	48. H	57. E	65. B
40. I	49. C	58. H	66. G
41. D	50. I	59. G	67. A
42. E	51. A	60. D	
43. G	52. F		

Chapters 26-31
68. B
69. E
70. D
71. A
72. C

DAILY LESSONS

LESSON ONE

Objectives
1. To introduce the *Mockingbird* unit
2. To distribute books and other related materials
3. To preview the study questions for chapters 1-3
4. To familiarize students with the vocabulary for chapters 1-3

Activity #1

Draw several figures on the board – a circle with some dots in the middle, a squiggly line, a square with two lines coming from it, two different sized rectangles adjacent to each other – any general figures that could be interpreted as several different things.

Have students take out a sheet of paper, and give them a few minutes to write down what each of the figures appears to be to them. Discuss their answers pointing out that a person's perspective or point of view influences how one perceives something. Two or more people can look at the same object and see two or more different things.

Transition: Point out that this is one thing to look for in *To Kill A Mockingbird*. Scout and Jem learn to "put themselves in other people's shoes," to try to see things from other people's perspectives, in order to begin to understand life and people.

Activity #2

Distribute the materials students will use in this unit. Explain in detail how students are to use these materials.

Study Guides Students should read the study guide questions for each reading assignment prior to beginning the reading assignment to get a feeling for what events and ideas are important in the section they are about to read. After reading the section, students will (as a class or individually) answer the questions to review the important events and ideas from that section of the book. Students should keep the study guides as study materials for the unit test.

Vocabulary Prior to reading a reading assignment, students will do vocabulary work related to the section of the book they are about to read. Following the completion of the reading of the book, there will be a vocabulary review of all the words used in the vocabulary assignments. Students should keep their vocabulary work as study materials for the unit test.

Reading Assignment Sheet You need to fill in the reading assignment sheet to let students know by when their reading has to be completed. You can either write the assignment sheet up on a side blackboard or bulletin board and leave it there for students to see each day, or you can "ditto" copies for each student to have. In either case, you should advise students to become very familiar with the reading assignments so they know what is expected of them.

<u>Extra Activities Center</u>   The Extra Activities Packet portion of this unit contains suggestions for an extra library of related books and articles in your classroom as well as crossword and word search puzzles. Make an extra activities center in your room where you will keep these materials for students to use. (Bring the books and articles in from the library and keep several copies of the puzzles on hand.) Explain to students that these materials are available for students to use when they finish reading assignments or other class work early.

<u>Nonfiction Assignment Sheet</u>   Explain to students that they each are to read at least one non-fiction piece from the in-class library at some time during the unit. Students will fill out a nonfiction assignment sheet after completing the reading to help you evaluate their reading experiences and to help the students think about and evaluate their own reading experiences.

<u>Books</u>   Each school has its own rules and regulations regarding student use of school books. Advise students of the procedures that are normal for your school.

<u>Activity #3</u>
Preview the study questions and have students do the vocabulary work for Chapters 1-3 of *To Kill A Mockingbird*. If students do not finish this assignment during this class period, they should complete it prior to the next class meeting.

NONFICTION ASSIGNMENT SHEET
(To be completed after reading the required nonfiction article)

Name _____ Date _____

Title of Nonfiction Read _____

Written By _____ Publication Date _____

I. Factual Summary: Write a short summary of the piece you read.

II. Vocabulary
    1. With which vocabulary words in the piece did you encounter some degree of difficulty?

    2. How did you resolve your lack of understanding with these words?

III. Interpretation: What was the main point the author wanted you to get from reading his work?

IV. Criticism
    1. With which points of the piece did you agree or find easy to accept? Why?

    2. With which points of the piece did you disagree or find difficult to believe? Why?

V. Personal Response: What do you think about this piece? OR How does this piece influence your ideas?

LESSON TWO

Objectives
1. To read chapters 1-3
2. To give students practice reading orally
3. To evaluate students' oral reading

Activity

    Have students read chapters 1-3 of *Mockingbird* out loud in class. You probably know the best way to get readers with your class; pick students at random, ask for volunteers, or use whatever method works best for your group. If you have not yet completed an oral reading evaluation for your students this marking period, this would be a good opportunity to do so. A form is included with this unit for your convenience.

    If students do not complete reading chapters 1-3 in class, they should do so prior to your next class meeting.

LESSON THREE

Objectives
1. To review the main events and ideas from chapters 1-3
2. To preview the study questions for chapters 4-7
3. To familiarize students with the vocabulary in chapters 4-7
4. To read chapters 4-7

Activity #1

    Give students a few minutes to formulate answers for the study guide questions for chapters 1-3, and then discuss the answers to the questions in detail. Write the answers on the board or overhead transparency so students can have the correct answers for study purposes.

Note: It is a good practice in public speaking and leadership skills for individual students to take charge of leading the discussions of the study questions. Perhaps a different student could go to the front of the class and lead the discussion each day that the study questions are discussed during this unit. Of course, the teacher should guide the discussion when appropriate and be sure to fill in any gaps the students leave.

Activity #2

    Give students about fifteen minutes to preview the study questions for chapters 4-7 of *Mockingbird* and to do the related vocabulary work.

Activity #3

    Assign students to read chapters 4-7 of *Mockingbird* prior to your next class period. If there is time remaining in this period, students may begin reading silently.

ORAL READING EVALUATION - *To Kill a Mockingbird*

Name _____ Class _____ Date _____

SKILL	EXCELLENT	GOOD	AVERAGE	FAIR	POOR
Fluency	5	4	3	2	1
Clarity	5	4	3	2	1
Audibility	5	4	3	2	1
Pronunciation	5	4	3	2	1
_____	5	4	3	2	1
_____	5	4	3	2	1

Total _____   Grade _____

Comments:

LESSON FOUR

Objectives
1. To check to see that students read chapters 4-7 as assigned
2. To review the main ideas and events from chapters 4-7
3. To preview the study questions for chapters 8-9
4. To familiarize students with the vocabulary in chapters 8-9
5. To read chapters 8-9
6. To evaluate students' oral reading

Activity #1

Quiz - Distribute quizzes and give students about 10 minutes to complete them.
(Note: The quizzes may either be the short answer study guides or the multiple choice version.) Have students exchange papers. Grade the quizzes as a class. Collect the papers for recording the grades.

Activity #2

Give students about 15 minutes to preview the study questions for chapters 8-9 and to do the related vocabulary work.

Activity #3

Have students read chapters 8-9 orally for the remainder of the class period. Continue the oral reading evaluations. If students do not complete reading these chapters during this class period, they should do so prior to your next class meeting.

LESSON FIVE

Objectives
1. To have students write a descriptive essay in a letter format
2. To give the teacher an opportunity to evaluate each student's writing skills
3. To give students an opportunity to produce an error-free paper and to apply the teacher's suggestions
4. To assign the pre-reading activities and the reading of chapters 10-11

Activity #1

Distribute Writing Assignment #1 and discuss the directions in detail. Allow the remaining class time for students to complete the assignment. Collect the papers at the end of the class period.

Activity #2

Tell students that prior to the next class period they should have previewed the study questions for, done the vocabulary for and read chapters 10-11. If they have time after completing the writing assignment, they may begin this reading assignment in class.

WRITING ASSIGNMENT #1 - *To Kill A Mockingbird*

PROMPT

Sometimes when you are talking to people or writing to a friend who has moved away, just relating the events which happen isn't enough. Sometimes you'll want to tell about a specific person or place in great detail; you'll want the person you're talking or writing to to see in his mind's eye exactly what you saw in real life. That's what DESCRIPTIVE essays or paragraphs are. The purpose is to describe someone or something as clearly and vividly as possible. You could just say, "I saw an adorable puppy at the pet shop." Your audience thinks of a generic adorable puppy. If, however, you go on to tell about the brown spots that look like dimples on either side of its mouth and the way one little pointy ear flips over at the tip or you tell how it hops up and down like a bunny when it is excited, you draw a more vivid picture of a specific puppy.

Your assignment is to write a descriptive essay focusing on Scout. Use a letter format; that will help you get started a little more quickly for this in-class assignment. Pretend you are Dill and write a letter home to your mother telling her about this person you've met - Jean Louise (Scout) Finch.

PREWRITING

A good way to start is to think of her physical appearance and jot down the characteristics which came to your mind. Next think of two other main personality characteristics. Jot those down. Beside each personality characteristic, jot down things she has done or said which have demonstrated those traits. Use your book if you have to for quick reference. You now have the makings for a least three paragraphs about your character: one for physical description and one each for two personality traits.

DRAFTING

You should begin your letter with an introductory paragraph, perhaps giving your mother some background about the fact that Scout and Jem are your neighbors, etc. Then you proceed with your three paragraphs.

It wouldn't seem quite right to just sign your name after these paragraphs. You should write a final paragraph in closing to tie things up so your reader isn't left saying, "So what?".

This is the format of a basic five paragraph essay. Introduce your topic, give three main points supported by examples or details and use the final paragraph to tie up the ideas and close the topic. Some essays will have more paragraphs in the body, depending on the complexity of the topic and the writing style of the author, but the basic idea remains the same.

PROMPT

When you finish the rough draft of your paper, ask a student who sits near you to read it. After reading your rough draft, he/she should tell you what he/she liked best about your work, which parts were difficult to understand, and ways in which your work could be improved. Reread your paper considering your critic's comments, and make the corrections you think are necessary.

LESSON SIX

Objectives
1. To review the main ideas of chapters 8-11
2. To preview the study questions for chapters 12-14
3. To read chapters 12-14

Activity #1
Ask students to get out their books and some paper (not their study guides). Tell students to write down ten questions (and answers) which cover the main events and ideas in chapters 8-11.

Discuss the students' questions and answers orally, making a list of the questions with brief responses on the board. Put a star next to the students' questions and answers that are essentially the same as the study guide questions. (Be sure that all the study guide questions are answered.)

Activity #2
Tell students to preview the study questions and do the vocabulary work for chapters 12-14.

Activity #3
Tell students that they should read chapters 12-14 prior to your next class meeting. If they have time after completing Activity #2, they may use the remainder of this class period to begin their reading.

LESSON SEVEN

Objectives
1. To review the main events of chapters 12-14
2. To check to see that students did the reading assignment
3. To assign the pre-reading, vocabulary and reading work for chapters 15-17 and 18-21

Activity #1
Give students a quiz on chapters 12-14. Use either the short answer or multiple choice form of the study guide questions as a quiz so that in discussing the answers to the quiz you also answer the study guide questions. Collect the papers for grade recording.

Activity #2
Tell students that prior to Lesson Nine they must have completed the pre-reading, vocabulary and reading work for chapters 15-17 and 18-21. Students may have the remainder of this period to work on this assignment.

LESSON EIGHT

Objectives
1. To evaluate students' writing
2. To have students revise their writing assignment 1 papers
3. To give students time to complete the assignment made in Lesson Seven

Activities

Call students to your desk (or some other private area) to discuss their papers from Writing Assignment 1. A Writing Evaluation Form is included with this unit to help structure your conferences.

While waiting to be called for a conference, students may work on the assignment made in Lesson Seven. After students have had a writing conference with you, they should return to their seats and begin working on their writing assignment revisions while your suggestions are fresh in their minds. Be sure to give students a day and a date for when their revisions are due.

LESSON NINE

Objectives
1. To review the main ideas and events of chapters 15-17 and 18-21
2. To preview the study questions for chapters 22-25
3. To do the vocabulary work for chapters 22-25
4. To read chapters 22-25
5. To complete the oral reading evaluations

Activity #1

Discuss the answers to the study guide questions for chapters 15-17 and 18-21. Write the answers on the board for students to copy down for study use later.

Activity #2

Give students about fifteen minutes to preview the study questions for chapters 22-25 and to complete the vocabulary work for those chapters.

Activity #3

Have students read chapters 22-25 orally in class. If you have not yet completed the oral reading evaluations, this is the time to do so.

Activity #4

Tell students that they are to complete the vocabulary work and the reading for chapters 26-31 prior to Lesson Eleven. (Give students a day and a date.)

WRITING EVALUATION FORM - *To Kill A Mockingbird*

Name _____ Date _____

Writing Assignment #1 for the *Mockingbird* unit   Grade _____

Circle One For Each Item:

Letter Format:	correct	errors noted on paper
Character Analysis:	excellent	good fair poor
Grammar:	correct	errors noted on paper
Spelling:	correct	errors noted on paper
Punctuation:	correct	errors noted on paper
Legibility:	excellent	good fair poor

Strengths:

Weaknesses:

Comments/Suggestions:

LESSON TEN

Objective
   To review all of the vocabulary work done in this unit

Activity
   Choose one (or more) of the vocabulary review activities listed below and spend your class period as directed in the activity. Some of the materials for these review activities are located in the Extra Activities Packet in this unit.

VOCABULARY REVIEW ACTIVITIES

1. Divide your class into two teams and have an old-fashioned spelling or definition bee.

2. Give each of your students (or students in groups of two, three or four) a *Mockingbird* Vocabulary Word Search Puzzle. The person (group) to find all of the vocabulary words in the puzzle first wins.

3. Give students a *Mockingbird* Vocabulary Word Search Puzzle without the word list. The person or group to find the most vocabulary words in the puzzle wins.

4. Use a *Mockingbird* Vocabulary Crossword Puzzle. Put the puzzle onto a transparency on the overhead projector (so everyone can see it), and do the puzzle together as a class.

5. Give students a *Mockingbird* Vocabulary Matching Worksheet to do.

6. Divide your class into two teams. Use the *Mockingbird* vocabulary words with their letters jumbled as a word list. Student 1 from Team A faces off against Student 1 from Team B. You write the first jumbled word on the board. The first student (1A or 1B) to unscramble the word wins the chance for his/her team to score points. If 1A wins the jumble, go to student 2A and give him/her a definition. He/she must give you the correct spelling of the vocabulary word which fits that definition. If he/she does, Team A scores a point, and you give student 3A a definition for which you expect a correctly spelled matching vocabulary word. Continue giving Team A definitions until some team member makes an incorrect response. An incorrect response sends the game back to the jumbled-word face off, this time with students 2A and 2B. Instead of repeating giving definitions to the first few students of each team, continue with the student after the one who gave the last incorrect response on the team. For example, if Team B wins the jumbled-word face-off, and student 5B gave the last incorrect answer for Team B, you would start this round of definition questions with student 6B, and so on. The team with the most points wins!

7. Have students write a story in which they correctly use as many vocabulary words as possible. Have students read their compositions orally! Post the most original compositions on your bulletin board!

LESSON ELEVEN

<u>Objectives</u>
    1. To review the main ideas and events from chapters 26-31
    2. To discuss *To Kill A Mockingbird* on interpretive and critical levels

<u>Activity #1</u>
    Take a few minutes at the beginning of the period to review the study questions for chapters 26-31.

<u>Activity #2</u>
    Choose the questions from the Extra Discussion Questions/Writing Assignments which seem most appropriate for your students. A class discussion of these questions is most effective if students have been given the opportunity to formulate answers to the questions prior to the discussion. To this end, you may either have all the students formulate answers to all the questions, divide your class into groups and assign one or more questions to each group, or you could assign one question to each student in your class. The option you choose will make a difference in the amount of class time needed for this activity.

<u>Activity #3</u>
    After students have had ample time to formulate answers to the questions, begin your class discussion of the questions and the ideas presented by the questions. Be sure students take notes during the discussion so they have information to study for the unit test.

EXTRA WRITING ASSIGNMENTS/DISCUSSION QUESTIONS - *Mockingbird*

Interpretation

1. Explain how Harper Lee's using Scout as the narrator affects our understanding of the events in *To Kill A Mockingbird*.

2. If you were to rewrite *To Kill A Mockingbird* as a play, where would you start and end each act? Explain why.

3. Explain how the two main story lines of the novel join together at the climax.

4. Explain why Arthur "Boo" Radley doesn't come out of the house except to help the children.

Critical

6. Describe Atticus' relationship with Jem and Scout and contrast it with their relationship to Aunt Alexandra.

7. Are Jem's actions believably motivated? Explain why or why not.

8. Explain the importance of the setting in *To Kill A Mockingbird*. Could this story have been set in a different time and place and still have the same effect?

9. Evaluate Harper Lee's style of writing. How does it contribute to the value of the novel?

10. Compare and contrast Atticus and Alexandra.

11. Compare and contrast Miss Maudie and Mrs. Dubose.

12. Explain how Harper Lee uses Mrs. Dubose and Boo Radley to develop the idea that things aren't always what they seem.

13. Explain how the title relates to the events of the novel and the themes of *To Kill A Mockingbird*.

14. Explain Dill's role in the novel. Why was he included?

15. Compare and contrast the Cunninghams and the Ewells.

16. Are the characters in *Mockingbird* stereotypes? If so, explain why Harper Lee used stereotypes. If not, explain how the characters merit individuality.

Mockingbird Extra Discussion Questions page 2

Critical/Personal Response

17. Could the same thing happen to Tom Robinson today? Explain why or why not.

18. Much of *To Kill A Mockingbird* tells about Scout's summer vacation time. Compare/contrast the activities of Scout's vacation with your own at Scout's age.

19. How would the story and its effect have changed if Jem and Scout had had a mother living?

20. Do you think the sibling relationship between Scout and Jem is realistic? Explain why or why not.

21. Who is responsible for Bob Ewell's death? (We know who killed him, but who is actually responsible in a broader sense, if anyone)?

22. Who is responsible for Tom Robinson's death?

23. Discuss the importance and the role of these characters in *Mockingbird*: Calpurnia, Dill, Mrs. Dubose, Miss Maudie, Miss Gates, Miss Caroline Fisher, Walter Cunningham, Dolphus Raymond, and Heck Tate.

24. Why did Atticus take Tom Robinson's case?

Personal Response

25. Did you enjoy reading *To Kill A Mockingbird*? Why or why not?

26. If Scout had written a poem about these childhood years, what would it have been? Write the poem as you think Scout would have written it.

27. Are there people in your neighborhood who are like any of the character types in the novel? Change the real person's name so his/her identity remains anonymous and describe how he or she is like a particular character.

28. Do you believe that Tom Robinson was shot while trying to escape from prison? Why or why not?

29. Why do kids (and sometimes grownups) pick on people like Boo Radley?

30. If Boo Radley were your neighbor, how would you feel about him? How would you act towards him?

31. Pretend you are a guide on a tour bus. Describe Maycomb as you drive through the streets.

Mockingbird Extra Discussion Questions page 3

32. What was "background" to Aunt Alexandra? Based on the information given in this book and on your own personal experiences, how would you define "background"?

33. What advantages do the children in this novel have over the adults?

34. Suppose this novel had been written from Atticus' point of view. How would the story have changed? From Cal's? From Boo Radley's? From Maudie's? Why do you think Harper Lee chose to write from Scout's point of view?

Quotations

1. "I maintain that the Ewells started it all, but Jem, who was four years my senior, said it started long before that. He said it began the summer Dill came to us, when Dill first gave us the idea of making Boo Radley come out."

2. "You're starting off on the wrong foot in every way, my dear. Hold out your hand." (Miss Fisher to Scout)

3. "You never really understand a person until you consider things from his point of view--. . . --until you climb into his skin and walk around in it."

4. "You are too young to understand it, ... but sometimes the Bible in the hand of one man is worse than a whiskey bottle in the hand of--oh, of your father."

5. "There are just some kind of men who--who're so busy worrying about the next world they've never learned to live in this one, and you can look down the street and see the results."

6. Miss Maudie looked around, and the shadow of her old grin crossed her face. "Always wanted a smaller house, Jem Finch. Gives me more yard. Just think, I'll have more room for my azaleas now!"

7. "Simply because we were licked a hundred years before we started is no reason for us not to try to win."

8. "Jack! When a child asks you something, answer him, for goodness' sake. But don't make a production of it. Children are children, but they can spot an evasion quicker than adults, and evasion simply muddles 'em."

9. "You're lucky, you know. You and Jem have the benefit of your father's age. If your father was thirty you'd find life quite different."

10. "The one thing that doesn't abide by majority rule is a person's conscience."

Mockingbird Extra Discussion Questions page 4

11. "I wanted you to see what real courage is, instead of getting the idea that courage is a man with a gun in his hand. It's when you know you're licked before you begin but you begin anyway and you see it through no matter what. You rarely win, but sometimes you do."

12. "Colored folks don't show their ages so fast," she said.
    "Maybe because they can't read. Cal, did you teach Zeebo?"

13. "It's not necessary to tell all you know. It's not lady-like--in the second place, folks don't like to have somebody around knowin' more than they do. It aggravates 'em."

14. "--good night, Atticus's gone all day and sometimes half the night and off in the legislature and I don't know what--you don't want 'em around all the time, Dill, you couldn't do anything if they were." (Scout to Dill)

15. "I'll tell him you said hey, little lady." (Mr. Cunningham to Scout)

16. ". . . you children last night made Walter Cunningham stand in my shoes for a minute. That was enough."

17. "The court appointed Atticus to defend him. Atticus aimed to defend him. That's what they didn't like about it. It was confusing."

18. "I try to give 'em a reason, you see. It helps folks if they can latch onto a reason."

19. "Cry about what, Mr. Raymond?" Dill's maleness was beginning to assert itself.
    "Cry about the simple hell people give other people--without even thinking."

20. "How could they do it, how could they?"
    "I don't know, but they did it. They've done it before and they did it tonight and they'll do it again and when they do it-- seems that only children weep. Good night." (Atticus to Jem)

21. "It's like bein' a caterpillar in a cocoon, that's what it is," he said. "Like somethin' asleep wrapped up in a warm place." (Jem about being a child in Maycomb)

22. "There ain't one thing in this world I can do about folks except laugh, so I'm gonna join the circus and laugh my head off."
    "You got it backwards, Dill," said Jem. "Clowns are sad, it's folks that laugh at them."
    "Well, I'm gonna be a new kind of clown. I'm gonna stand in the middle of the ring and laugh at the folks. Just looks yonder," he pointed. "Every one of 'em oughta be ridin' broomsticks."

Mockingbird Extra Discussion Questions page 5

23. "Our stout Maycomb citizens aren't interested, in the first place. In the second place, they're afraid."

24. "Serving on a jury forces a man to make up his mind and declare himself about something. Men don't like to do that. Sometimes it's unpleasant."

25. "Whether Maycomb knows it or not, we're paying the highest tribute we can pay a man. We trust him to do right. It's that simple."

26. "After all, if Aunty could be a lady at a time like this, so could I."

27. "So many things had happened to us, Boo Radley was the least of our fears."

28. "Tom was a dead man the minute Mayella Ewell opened her mouth and screamed."

29. ". . . things had a way of settling down, and after enough time passed people would forget that Tom Robinson's existence was ever brought to their attention."

30. "As it was, we were compelled to hold our heads high and be, respectively, a gentleman and a lady. In a way, it was like the era of Mrs. Henry Lafayette Dubose, without all her yelling."

31. "Jem how can you hate Hitler so bad an' then turn around and be ugly about folks right at home--" (Scout to Jem about Miss Gates)

32. "Let the dead bury the dead this time, Mr. Finch."

33. "We never put back into the tree what we took out of it: we had given him nothing, and it made me sad."

LESSON TWELVE

Objectives
1. To complete the discussions begun in Lesson Eleven
2. To discuss the further development of the themes of the novel
3. To give students a chance to work together in small groups to exchange ideas and find information

Activity #1
Complete any discussions not done in Lesson Eleven.

Activity #2
Divide your class into 6 groups - one group for each theme: education, bravery/cowardice, race prejudice, social class prejudice, sex prejudice, and respect of the individual. Allow the groups time to find specific examples of their theme in the novel. The groups should assign so-many chapters per person to look for specific examples and write them down. Allow time for the group members to discuss their findings and come up with some intelligent statement about the theme in the novel so far. The groups should appoint a spokesperson to report the group's thoughts.

LESSON THIRTEEN

Objectives
1. To discuss the major themes in the novel
2. To allow students time to review, compare and correct their notes

Activity #1
Use the groups' work as a nucleus and a springboard for discussions about the major themes in the novel. Call on individual group members by chapter(s) to give the examples they found of their theme in those chapters. Jot them down briefly for students to copy into their notes. Ask the group spokesperson to give the group's thoughts about the theme development so far. Jot these down. Ask if anyone from the group has anything to add. Take the time to discuss each theme thoroughly with the class and be sure to allow time for students (either members of the group or other class members) to express their ideas or ask questions.

NOTE: Having students report in this manner takes a little longer than having just one student from each group report, but it holds all group members accountable for their work.

Activity #2
Allow any remaining time for students to review, compare and/or correct their notes.

LESSON FOURTEEN

Objectives
1. To give students the opportunity to practice writing to persuade
2. To give students the chance to think in detail about at least one of the themes in *To Kill A Mockingbird*
3. To give the teacher a chance to evaluate students' individual writing
4. To give students the opportunity to correct their writing errors and produce an error-free paper

Activity

Distribute Writing Assignment #2. Discuss the directions orally in detail. Allow the remaining class time for students to complete the activity.

If students do not have enough class time to finish, the papers may be collected at the beginning of the next class period.

Follow-Up: Follow up by allowing students to correct their errors and turn in the revision for credit. A good time for your next writing conferences would be the day following the unit test.

WRITING ASSIGNMENT #2 *To Kill A Mockingbird*

PROMPT

This writing assignment is to give you practice writing an essay outside of the letter format and to give you a chance to express your views regarding one of the themes we've been discussing in *To Kill A Mockingbird*.

The assignment is to write a five paragraph essay about one of the themes in the novel. You can find some good ideas for topics from your class notes. Pick any conclusion the class found for any theme, and you will have a pretty good topic for an essay.

PREWRITING

One way to start is to jot down ideas relevant to your topic. Then, on your scratch paper, pick out your three best points. Organize any other thoughts you've put down to see if they can be used as supporting examples or statements for any of your three main points. Scratch out anything that's left. Now go back and jot down any more ideas you have which will support your three ideas.

DRAFTING

A diagram of a basic, five-paragraph essay might look like this:

¶1. Introduce essay topic
¶2. Main Idea (topic sentence) followed by examples or details supporting main idea
¶3. Main idea (topic sentence) followed by examples or details supporting main idea
¶4. Main idea (topic sentence) followed by examples or details supporting main idea
¶5. Summary/Closing

Once you have mastered the basic skills of making a main topic, supporting that main topic with main ideas of substance and explaining those main ideas with examples or details, a whole new world of creativity in writing opens up for you. It is then you can perfect your style of writing, choosing a <u>way of delivering</u> your ideas.

PROMPT

When you finish the rough draft of your paper, ask a student who sits near you to read it. After reading your rough draft, he/she should tell you what he/she liked best about your work, which parts were difficult to understand, and ways in which your work could be improved. Reread your paper considering your critic's comments, and make the corrections you think are necessary.

PROOFREADING

Do a final proofreading of your paper double-checking your grammar, spelling, organization, and the clarity of your ideas.

LESSON FIFTEEN

Objectives
1. To widen the breadth of students' knowledge about the topics discussed or touched upon in *To Kill A Mockingbird*
2. To check students' nonfiction reading assignments

Activity
Ask each student to give a brief oral report about the nonfiction work he/she read for the nonfiction reading assignment. Your criteria for evaluating this report will vary depending on the level of your students. You may wish for students to give a complete report without using notes of any kind, or you may want students to read directly from a written report, or you may want to do something in between these two extremes. Just make students aware of your criteria in ample time for them to prepare their reports.

Start with one student's report. After that, ask if anyone else in the class has read about a topic related to the first student's report. If no one has, choose another student at random. After each report, be sure to ask if anyone has a report related to the one just completed. That will help keep a continuity during the discussion of the reports.

LESSON SIXTEEN

Objectives
1. To have students take their knowledge of all of the major elements of *Mockingbird* beyond the pages of the book
2. To give students the opportunity to express their personal opinions and use their creativity
3. To have students work together as a group for a common purpose
4. To have students practice evaluating suggestions, choosing the best suggestions, and compromising when necessary

Activity
The teacher will lead the class in a group writing activity. The whole class will participate in writing one of the following assignments:

A. Write a plot summary of *To Kill A Mockingbird II*.

OR B. Change the time and setting of *To Kill A Mockingbird* to a city in the 1990's, and write a plot summary as you think the story would be told.

IF YOU CHOOSE "A", students should decide on how much time has passed since "*Mockingbird I*" has taken place. One way to then tackle the writing assignment is for students to decide what would logically happen to each character in the sequel. After you do a character or two, you will probably find the characters interacting with each other (what one does affects another). If your students aren't inclined to "jump in and run" with this assignment, start by asking specific students specific questions. For example, Student A, what do you think Scout would do in the sequel? Student B, do you agree with Student A, or do you think Scout would do something different? Jot down the events upon which your students decide, and use that as a rough draft from which to write. Have students give you specific sentences to write in your plot summary. Review and revise the summary as a class until you have a good, finished product.

IF YOU CHOOSE B, one way to begin is to make a list of the major elements of the original story. Which major events and characters need to be considered in the "updated" version of the book? From this, work out a "--- should be changed to ----" kind of list showing how each of the major events or characters will need to be changed. From that, have students work out a story line. Write that down on the board. From the story line, have students give you specific sentences to write into a plot summary. Review and revise the plot summary until you have a good, finished product.

LESSON SEVENTEEN

Objective
To review the main ideas presented in *To Kill A Mockingbird*

Activity #1
Choose one of the review games/activities included in the packet and spend your class period as outlined there. Some materials for these activities are located in the Extra Activities section of this unit.

Activity #2
Remind students that the Unit Test will be in the next class meeting. Stress the review of the Study Guides and their class notes as a last minute, brush-up review for homework.

REVIEW GAMES/ACTIVITIES - *To Kill A Mockingbird*

1. Ask the class to make up a unit test for *To Kill A Mockingbird*. The test should have 4 sections: matching, true/false, short answer, and essay. Students may use 1/2 period to make the test and then swap papers and use the other 1/2 class period to take a test a classmate has devised. (open book) You may want to use the unit test included in this packet or take questions from the students' unit tests to formulate your own test.

2. Take 1/2 period for students to make up true and false questions (including the answers). Collect the papers and divide the class into two teams. Draw a big tic-tac-toe board on the chalk board. Make one team X and one team O. Ask questions to each side, giving each student one turn. If the question is answered correctly, that students' team's letter (X or O) is placed in the box. If the answer is incorrect, no mark is placed in the box. The object is to get three marks in a row like tic-tac-toe. You may want to keep track of the number of games won for each team.

3. Take 1/2 period for students to make up questions (true/false and short answer). Collect the questions. Divide the class into two teams. You'll alternate asking questions to individual members of teams A & B (like in a spelling bee). The question keeps going from A to B until it is correctly answered, then a new question is asked. A correct answer does not allow the team to get another question. Correct answers are +2 points; incorrect answers are -1 point.

4. Have students pair up and quiz each other from their study guides and class notes.

5. Give students a *Mockingbird* crossword puzzle to complete.

6. Divide your class into two teams. Use the *Mockingbird* crossword words with their letters jumbled as a word list. Student 1 from Team A faces off against Student 1 from Team B. You write the first jumbled word on the board. The first student (1A or 1B) to unscramble the word wins the chance for his/her team to score points. If 1A wins the jumble, go to student 2A and give him/her a clue. He/she must give you the correct word which matches that clue. If he/she does, Team A scores a point, and you give student 3A a clue for which you expect another correct response. Continue giving Team A clues until some team member makes an incorrect response. An incorrect response sends the game back to the jumbled-word face off, this time with students 2A and 2B. Instead of repeating giving clues to the first few students of each team, continue with the student after the one who gave the last incorrect response on the team. For example, if Team B wins the jumbled-word face-off, and student 5B gave the last incorrect answer for Team B, you would start this round of clue questions with student 6B, and so on. The team with the most points wins!

UNIT TESTS

SHORT ANSWER UNIT TEST 1 - *To Kill A Mockingbird*

I. Matching/Identify

_____ 1. Atticus Finch   A. presiding judge at the trial
_____ 2. Scout   B. Atticus' sister
_____ 3. Jem   C. Scout's brother
_____ 4. Calpurnia   D. lawyer who defends a Negro
_____ 5. Aunt Alexandra   E. old lady who yells at the children
_____ 6. Dill   F. narrator
_____ 7. Judge Taylor   G. summertime neighbor of the Finch children
_____ 8. Miss Maudie   H. mysterious neighbor
_____ 9. Mrs. Dubose   I. the sheriff
_____ 10. Arthur (Boo) Radley   J. attacks the children
_____ 11. Tom Robinson   K. open-minded neighbor friendly to the children
_____ 12. Heck Tate   L. the cook
_____ 13. Bob Ewell   M. she was allegedly raped
_____ 14. Mayella Ewell   N. the defendant on trial for rape
_____ 15. Walter Cunningham (Sr.) O. farmer who won't take charity
_____ 16. Rev. Sykes   P. gossipy neighbor
_____ 17. Stephanie Crawford   Q. the prosecuting attorney
_____ 18. Caroline Fisher   R. pretends to be a drunk
_____ 19. Mr. Gilmer   S. Cal's preacher
_____ 20. Dolphus Raymond   T. first grade teacher

II. Short Answer

1. What did Miss Maudie think of the Radleys?

2. What was the Boo Radley game?

3. How did Jem lose his pants? What did he find when he went back for them?

Mockingbird Short Answer Unit Test 1 Page 2

4. What brave thing did Atticus do in Chapter 10? Why were Jem and Scout shocked?

5. What did Jem do when Mrs. Dubose said Atticus "lawed for niggers?" What was his punishment?

6. "Aunt Alexandra fitted into the world of Maycomb like a hand in a glove, but she never fitted into the world of Jem and me." Explain.

7. Why did Cunningham's mob leave?

8. What was Tom's handicap, and why was it important to his case?

9. What did Scout and Dill learn from Mr. Dolphus Raymond?

10. Why did Jem cry after he heard the jury's verdict?

Mockingbird Short Answer Unit Test 1 Page 3

11. Jem said, " I think I'm beginning to understand why Boo Radley's stayed shut up in the house all this time . . . it's because he wants to stay inside." Explain.

12. What happened to Jem and Scout on the way home from the pageant?

13. Who saved Jem and Scout, and who killed Bob Ewell?

14. Why did Heck Tate insist that Bob Ewell fell on his own knife?

15. Scout arranged things so that "if Miss Stephanie Crawford was watching from her upstairs window, she would see Arthur Radley escorting [her] down the sidewalk, as any gentleman would do." Why?

Mockingbird Short Answer Unit Test 1 Page 4

III. Essay

Scout and Jem learn that one must have respect for individuals. Explain how they learned about respect for the individual from Boo Radley, Mrs. Dubose, Atticus, Mr. Raymond, Cal, Aunt Alexandra, and Tom Robinson.

Mockingbird Short Answer Unit Test 1 Page 5

IV. Vocabulary

Listen to the vocabulary word and spell it.
After you have spelled all the words, go back and write down the definition.

1.

2.

3.

4.

5.

6.

7.

8.

9.

10.

SHORT ANSWER UNIT TEST 2 - *To Kill A Mockingbird*

I. Matching

___	1. Atticus Finch	A.	she was allegedly raped
___	2. Scout	B.	the defendant on trial for rape
___	3. Jem	C.	farmer who won't take charity
___	4. Calpurnia	D.	gossipy neighbor
___	5. Aunt Alexandra	E.	the prosecuting attorney
___	6. Dill	F.	pretends to be a drunk
___	7. Judge Taylor	G.	Cal's preacher
___	8. Miss Maudie	H.	first grade teacher
___	9. Mrs. Dubose	I.	presiding judge at the trial
___	10. Arthur (Boo) Radley	J.	Atticus' sister
___	11. Tom Robinson	K.	Scout's brother
___	12. Heck Tate	L.	lawyer who defends Tom
___	13. Bob Ewell	M.	old lady who yells at the children
___	14. Mayella Ewell	N.	narrator
___	15. Walter Cunningham, Sr.	O.	summertime neighbor of the Finch children
___	16. Rev. Sykes	P.	mysterious neighbor
___	17. Stephanie Crawford	Q.	the sheriff
___	18. Caroline Fisher	R.	attacks the children
___	19. Mr. Gilmer	S.	open-minded neighbor friendly to the children
___	20. Dolphus Raymond	T.	the cook

Mockingbird Short Answer Unit Test 2 page 2
II. Short Answer
1. Scout said, " He ain't company, Cal, he's just a Cunningham." What did she mean by that and what was Cal's answer?

2. Why do Dill and Jem want to give Boo Radley a note? What does Atticus say when he finds out about their plan?

3. What happened to Miss Maudie's house? What was her reaction?

4. What did Scout's Uncle Jack learn from Scout and Atticus?

5. What did Jem learn from his encounter with Mrs. Dubose and following her death?

6. How does Jem change during the course of the story?

7. Atticus and Alexandra disagree about how to deal with the children. How does Atticus handle the situation?

Mockingbird Short Answer Unit Test 2 page 3

8. What was the importance of Mayella's bruises being primarily on the right-hand side of her face?

9. What were Atticus' closing remarks to the jury?

10. Alexandra doesn't want Scout playing with Walter Cunningham. Why not?

11. What was Scout's fantasy regarding Arthur (Boo) Radley?

12. As Scout leaves the Radley porch, she looks out at the neighborhood and recounts the events of the last few years from the Radleys' perspective. Why is that important?

Mockingbird Short Answer Unit Test 2 page 4

III. Composition

Choose a different title for *To Kill A Mockingbird* and explain how your title is appropriate, considering the themes and ideas presented in the novel.

Mockingbird Short Answer Unit Test 2 page 5

IV. Vocabulary

> Listen to the vocabulary word and spell it.
> After you have spelled all the words, go back and write down the definitions.

1.

2.

3.

4.

5.

6.

7.

8.

9.

10.

KEY: SHORT ANSWER UNIT TESTS - *To Kill A Mockingbird*

The short answer questions are taken directly from the study guides.
If you need to look up the answers, you will find them in the study guide section.

Answers to the composition questions will vary depending on your
class discussions and the level of your students.

For the vocabulary section of the test, choose ten of the
words from the vocabulary lists to read orally for your students.

The answers to the matching section of the test are below.

Answers to the matching section of the Advanced Short Answer Unit Test
are the same as for Short Answer Unit Test #2.

Test #1	Test #2
1. D	1. L
2. F	2. N
3. C	3. K
4. L	4. T
5. B	5. J
6. G	6. O
7. A	7. I
8. K	8. S
9. E	9. M
10. H	10. P
11. N	11. B
12. I	12. Q
13. J	13. R
14. M	14. A
15. O	15. C
16. S	16. G
17. P	17. D
18. T	18. H
19. Q	19. E
20. R	20. F

ADVANCED SHORT ANSWER UNIT TEST - *To Kill A Mockingbird*

I. Matching

___ 1. Atticus Finch   A. she was allegedly raped

___ 2. Scout   B. the defendant on trial for rape

___ 3. Jem   C. farmer who won't take charity

___ 4. Calpurnia   D. gossipy neighbor

___ 5. Aunt Alexandra   E. the prosecuting attorney

___ 6. Dill   F. pretends to be a drunk

___ 7. Judge Taylor   G. Cal's preacher

___ 8. Miss Maudie   H. first grade teacher

___ 9. Mrs. Dubose   I. presiding judge at the trial

___ 10. Arthur (Boo) Radley   J. Atticus' sister

___ 11. Tom Robinson   K. Scout's brother

___ 12. Heck Tate   L. lawyer who defends Tom

___ 13. Bob Ewell   M. old lady who yells at the children

___ 14. Mayella Ewell   N. narrator

___ 15. Walter Cunningham, Sr. O. summertime neighbor of the Finch children

___ 16. Rev. Sykes   P. mysterious neighbor

___ 17. Stephanie Crawford   Q. the sheriff

___ 18. Caroline Fisher   R. attacks the children

___ 19. Mr. Gilmer   S. open-minded neighbor friendly to the children

___ 20. Dolphus Raymond   T. the cook

Mockingbird Advanced Short Answer Unit Test page 2
II. Short Answer

1. Explain how Harper Lee's using Scout as the narrator affects our understanding of the events in the novel.

2. Explain how the two main story lines of the novel join together at the climax.

3. Describe Atticus' relationship with Jem and Scout and contrast it with their relationship to Aunt Alexandra.

4. Explain how Harper Lee uses Mrs. Dubose and Boo Radley to develop the idea that things aren't always what they seem.

5. Discuss the importance and role of these characters in *Mockingbird*: Calpurnia, Dill, Miss Maudie, Walter Cunningham, and Dolphus Raymond.

Mockingbird Advanced Short Answer Unit Test page 3

III. Quotations: Explain the importance and meaning of the following quotations:

1. "You never really understand a person until you consider things from his point of view--...-- until you climb into his skin and walk around in it."

2. "How could they do it, how could they"?
   "I don't know, but they did it. They've done it before and they did it tonight and they'll do it again and when they do it--seems that only children weep."

3. "There ain't one thing in this world I can do about folks except laugh, so I'm gonna join the circus and laugh my head off. . . . I'm gonna be a new kind of clown. I'm gonna stand in the middle of the ring and laugh at the folks. Just look yonder. . . . Every one of 'em oughta be ridin' broomsticks."

4. "Tom was a dead man the minute Mayella Ewell opened her mouth and screamed."

5. "Let the dead bury the dead this time, Mr. Finch."

Mockingbird Advanced Short Answer Unit Test page 4

IV. Vocabulary

Listen to the vocabulary words and write them down. After you have written down all the words, write a paragraph using all of the vocabulary words. The paragraph must in some way relate to *To Kill A Mockingbird*.

MULTIPLE CHOICE UNIT TEST 1 - *To Kill A Mockingbird*

I. Matching

1. Atticus Finch
2. Scout
3. Jem
4. Calpurnia
5. Aunt Alexandra
6. Dill
7. Judge Taylor
8. Miss Maudie
9. Mrs. Dubose
10. Arthur (Boo) Radley
11. Tom Robinson
12. Heck Tate
13. Bob Ewell
14. Mayella Ewell
15. Walter Cunningham, Sr.
16. Rev. Sykes
17. Stephanie Crawford
18. Caroline Fisher
19. Mr. Gilmer
20. Dolphus Raymond

A. presiding judge at the trial
B. Atticus' sister
C. Scout's brother
D. lawyer who defends a Negro
E. old lady who yells at the children
F. narrator
G. summertime neighbor of the Finch children
H. mysterious neighbor
I. the sheriff
J. attacks the children
K. open-minded neighbor friendly to the children
L. the cook
M. she was allegedly raped
N. the defendant on trial for rape
O. farmer who won't take charity
P. gossipy neighbor
Q. the prosecuting attorney
R. pretends to be a drunk
S. Cal's preacher
T. first grade teacher

II. Multiple Choice

1. What does Miss Maudie think of the Radleys?
    a. They have a right to their privacy.
    b. They all need a bath.
    c. She is afraid of them.
    d. They should all be locked away.

2. How did Jem lose his pants?
    a. Boo Radley stole them.
    b. Miss Maudie took them to mend without telling him.
    c. Scout played a trick on him.
    d. He took them off to free himself from the fence.

3. Describe the relationship between Aunt Alexandra and the children.
    a. They were good friends.
    b. Alexandra was like their teacher.
    c. Alexandra was just like Atticus to them.
    d. They were usually at odds with each other

Mockingbird Multiple Choice Unit Test 1 Page 2

4. Why did Dill run away from home back to Maycomb?
    a. He hated his foster home.
    b. He secretly knew he should testify on behalf of Mr. Robinson.
    c. He didn't feel like his parents needed him.
    d. Boo needed him.

5. What do Dill and Scout learn from Mr. Raymond?
    a. Crime doesn't pay.
    b. People aren't always as they appear to be.
    c. Mobs don't solve anything.
    d. Some people never learn.

6. What were Atticus' closing remarks to the jury?
    a. There was no medical evidence to suggest that Mayella had been raped.
    b. Tom Robinson was a drunk, but really innocent.
    c. Mayella was crazy and should be the one being locked away.
    d. All of the above

7. Why did Jem cry?
    a. Tom was his best friend.
    b. Aunt Alexandra was leaving.
    c. He was shocked at the injustice of the jury.
    d. People were making fun of Atticus.

8. What was the significance of Maudie's two little cakes and one large one?
    a. Dill and Scout had earned cakes of their own.
    b. Jem had graduated from childhood.
    c. The big piece was Scout's reward.
    d. Maudie just didn't have enough little cakes.

9. Alexandra doesn't want Scout playing with Walter Cunningham. Why not?
    a. Walter is a bad boy.
    b. She is afraid of him.
    c. Cunninghams are not social equals of the Finches.
    d. Scout has been grounded.

10. Why does Jem think Boo stays inside?
    a. The outside world is too complicated.
    b. He is forced to against his will.
    c. for medical reasons
    d. He is crazy.

Mockingbird Multiple Choice Unit Test 1 Page 3

11. What was Scout's fantasy regarding Arthur (Boo) Radley?
    a. She would rescue Boo.
    b. Boo would be lynched by a mob.
    c. Boo would run away with Tom Robinson, and they would both be safe.
    d. Boo would be normal.

12. What happened to Jem and Scout on the way home from the pageant?
    a. They got lost.
    b. They got run over.
    c. Someone attacked them.
    d. They were kidnaped.

13. Why did Heck Tate insist that Bob Ewell fell on his own knife?
    a. To cover up for himself
    b. To cover up for Boo
    c. To cover up for Tom Robinson
    d. Because he did

III. True or False?

1. Miss Maudie left fires going (for warmth) and her house burned down. She was devastated by the fire and the loss of her home, and never quite recovered.

2. Cecil Jacobs was a boy at Scout's school who made Scout aware that Atticus was defending a black man.

3. Scout agreed with Francis' attitude towards Atticus' case.

4. Jem had to read to Miss Maudie each afternoon after school for a month.

5. Atticus hated Boo Radley.

6. Heck Tate's mob wanted to get Tom Robinson and inflict their own justice on him.

7. Scout saved Atticus and Mr. Robinson from a mob.

8. Scout wanted Boo Radley to be normal.

9. Helen Robinson was a troublemaker.

10. Miss Gates was a hypocrite.

Mockingbird Multiple Choice Unit Test 1 Page 4

III. Composition

    Scout and Jem learn that one must have respect for individuals. Explain how they learned about respect for the individual from Boo Radley, Mrs. Dubose, Atticus, Mr. Raymond, Cal, Aunt Alexandra, and Tom Robinson.

Mockingbird Multiple Choice Unit Test 1 Page 5

IV. Vocabulary: Multiple choice. Write in the letter of the word that matches the definition.
1. Supposedly; believed to be so but not yet proved
  A. persecuted B. desolate C. fraud D. allegedly
2. To go against
  A. contradict B. subtlety C. extract D. sustain
3. Evaluation
  A. desolate B. acquired C. assessment D. tyranny
4. Unavoidable; bound to happen
  A. inaudible B. defendant C. inevitable D. sustain
5. Something not obvious
  A. malignant B. pursuit C. desolate D. subtlety
6. Authoritative statements
  A. pronouncements B. indigenous C. acquiescences D. hypocrites
7. Settlement of differences in which concessions are made
  A. encumbered B. sustain C. compromise D. irked
8. Incur the dislike of someone; counteract
  A. pursuit B. fraud C. indulge D. antagonize
9. Made familiar with
  A. meditative B. cantankerous C. acquainted D. emerge
10. Coming after
  A. antagonize B. subsequent C. inconveniences D. pauper
11. Poor person
  A. peril B. pauper C. obscure D. desolate
12. Thoughtful
  A. cantankerous B. pensive C. infallible D. inevitable
13. To allow oneself a special pleasure
  A. irked B. eccentric C. antagonize D. indulge
14. Person against whom an action is brought
  A. pauper B. chameleon C. defendant D. eccentric
15. Deliberate deception for unfair or unlawful gain
  A. compromise B. fraud C. pursuits D. subtlety
16. Given over to another for care or protection
  A. adjacent B. begrudge C. entrusted D. obscure
17. Unable to be heard
  A. inaudible B. infallible C. adjacent D. acquainted
18. Harassing; bothering; pestering
  A. subsequent B. encumbered C. tormenting D. cantankerous
19. Not readily noticeable
  A. inconspicuous B. infallible C. eccentric D. chameleon
20. Obtained
  A. acquainted B. acquired C. entrusted D. antagonized

MULTIPLE CHOICE UNIT TEST 2 - *To Kill A Mockingbird*

I. Matching

1. Atticus Finch
2. Scout
3. Jem
4. Calpurnia
5. Aunt Alexandra
6. Dill
7. Judge Taylor
8. Miss Maudie
9. Mrs. Dubose
10. Arthur (Boo) Radley
11. Tom Robinson
12. Heck Tate
13. Bob Ewell
14. Mayella Ewell
15. Walter Cunningham, Sr.
16. Rev. Sykes
17. Stephanie Crawford
18. Caroline Fisher
19. Mr. Gilmer
20. Dolphus Raymond

A. she was allegedly raped
B. the defendant on trial for rape
C. farmer who won't take charity
D. gossipy neighbor
E. the prosecuting attorney
F. pretends to be a drunk
G. Cal's preacher
H. first grade teacher
I. presiding judge at the trial
J. Atticus' sister
K. Scout's brother
L. lawyer who defends Tom
M. old lady who yells at the children
N. narrator
O. summertime neighbor of the Finch children
P. mysterious neighbor
Q. the sheriff
R. attacks the children
S. open-minded neighbor friendly to the children
T. the cook

II. Multiple Choice

1. What does Miss Maudie think of the Radleys?
    a. She is afraid of them.
    b. They all need a bath.
    c. They have a right to their privacy.
    d. They should all be locked away.

2. How did Jem lose his pants?
    a. Boo Radley stole them.
    b. Miss Maudie took them to mend without telling him.
    c. He took them off to free himself from the fence.
    d. Scout played a trick on him.

3. Describe the relationship between Aunt Alexandra and the children.
    a. They were usually at odds with each other
    b. Alexandra was like their teacher.
    c. Alexandra was just like Atticus to them.
    d. They were good friends.

Mockingbird Multiple Choice Unit Test 2 Page 2

4. Why did Dill run away from home back to Maycomb?
    a. He didn't feel like his parents needed him.
    b. He secretly knew he should testify on behalf of Mr. Robinson.
    c. He hated his foster home.
    d. Boo needed him.

5. What do Dill and Scout learn from Mr. Raymond?
    a. Crime doesn't pay.
    b. Some people never learn.
    c. Mobs don't solve anything.
    d. People aren't always as they appear to be.

6. What were Atticus' closing remarks to the jury?
    a. C & D
    b. Tom Robinson was a drunk, but really innocent.
    c. Mayella was crazy and should be the one being locked away.
    d. There was no medical evidence to suggest that Mayella had been raped.

7. Why did Jem cry?
    a. Tom was his best friend.
    b. Aunt Alexandra was leaving.
    c. He was shocked at the injustice of the jury.
    d. People were making fun of Atticus.

8. What was the significance of Maudie's two little cakes and one large one?
    a. Dill and Scout had earned cakes of their own.
    b. Jem had graduated from childhood.
    c. The big piece was Scout's reward.
    d. Maudie just didn't have enough little cakes.

9. Alexandra doesn't want Scout playing with Walter Cunningham. Why not?
    a. Cunninghams are not social equals of the Finches.
    b. She is afraid of him.
    c. Walter is a bad boy.
    d. Scout has been grounded.

10. Why does Jem think Boo stays inside?
    a. Medical reasons
    b. He is forced to against his will.
    c. The outside world is too complicated.
    d. He is crazy.

Mockingbird Multiple Choice Unit Test 2 Page 3

11. What was Scout's fantasy regarding Arthur (Boo) Radley?
 a. She would rescue Boo.
 b. Boo would be normal.
 c. Boo would run away with Tom Robinson, and they would both be safe.
 d. Boo would be lynched by a mob.

12. What happened to Jem and Scout on the way home from the pageant?
 a. They got lost.
 b. They got run over.
 c. They were kidnapped.
 d. Someone attacked them.

13. Why did Heck Tate insist that Bob Ewell fell on his own knife?
 a. to cover up for Boo
 b. to cover up for himself
 c. to cover up for Tom Robinson
 d. because he did

III. True or False?

 1. Miss Maudie left fires going (for warmth) and her house burned down. Because Jem started the fire, even though it was an accident, he had to go to her house every day after school for a month.

 2. Cecil Jacobs was a boy who had cooties.

 3. Scout disagreed with Francis' attitude towards Atticus' case.

 4. Jem cut down Miss Maudie's bushes.

 5. The jury brought back a verdict that was just and fair considering the evidence.

 6. Heck Tate attacked the children on their way home from the school pageant.

 7. Scout saved Atticus and Mr. Robinson from a mob.

 8. Aunt Alexandria was a nasty old woman who just wanted to cause trouble for the children.

 9. Helen Robinson was a troublemaker.

 10. Miss Gates was a hypocrite.

Mockingbird Multiple Choice Unit Test 2 Page 4

IV. Composition

Choose a different title for *To Kill A Mockingbird* and explain how your title is appropriate, considering the themes and ideas presented in the novel.

Mockingbird Multiple Choice Unit Test 2 Page 5

V. Vocabulary: Multiple choice. Write in the letter of the word that matches the definition.

1. Good-naturedly; cordially
    A. inevitably   B. amiably   C. pensive   D. subtlety
2. Pertaining to church
    A. ecclesiastical   B. subsequent   C. malignant   D. pauper
3. Something not obvious
    A. intimidation   B. subsequent   C. subtlety   D. pensive
4. Characterized by secret movement; avoiding notice
    A. stealthy   B. dispelled   C. condescended   D. malignant
5. In complete agreement
    A. persevere   B. evasion   C. unanimous   D. emerge
6. Unable to be heard
    A. eccentric   B. inaudible   C. inevitable   D. dispelled
7. Harassing; bothering; pestering
    A. malevolent   B. tormenting   C. stealthy   D. malignant
8. Unaware
    A. stealthy   B. pensive   C. oblivious   D. inaudible
9. Deliberating; considering
    A. tormenting   B. cantankerous   C. debating   D. prejudice
10. Annoyed; bothered
    A. begrudged   B. pensive   C. cantankerous   D. irked
11. Made familiar with
    A. acquainted   B. ascertained   C. oblivious   D. unanimous
12. Without sophistication; artless; innocent
    A. subtlety   B. ingenuous   C. preoccupation   D. inaudible
13. Danger
    A. tyranny   B. intimidation   C. peril   D. malevolent
14. Extreme harshness; rigor
    A. tyranny   B. intimidation   C. peril   D. evasion
15. Preconceived preference or idea; bias
    A. ingenuous   B. prejudice   C. peril   D. evasion
16. Threats
    A. tyranny   B. peril   C. intimidation   D. fraud
17. To allow one a special pleasure
    A. indulge   B. intimidate   C. prejudice   D. acquire
18. To have done away with
    A. acquired   B. torment   C. dispelled   D. indulged
19. Remain constant to a purpose in spite of obstacles
    A. ascertain   B. indulge   C. emerge   D. persevere
20. To keep in existence; maintain; prolong
    A. emerge   B. sustain   C. indulge   D. torment

ANSWER SHEET - *To Kill A Mockingbird*
Multiple Choice Unit Tests

I. Matching	II. Multiple Choice	III. True or False	IV. Vocabulary
1. ___	1. ___	1. ___	1. ___
2. ___	2. ___	2. ___	2. ___
3. ___	3. ___	3. ___	3. ___
4. ___	4. ___	4. ___	4. ___
5. ___	5. ___	5. ___	5. ___
6. ___	6. ___	6. ___	6. ___
7. ___	7. ___	7. ___	7. ___
8. ___	8. ___	8. ___	8. ___
9. ___	9. ___	9. ___	9. ___
10. ___	10. ___	10. ___	10. ___
11. ___	11. ___		11. ___
12. ___	12. ___		12. ___
13. ___	13. ___		13. ___
14. ___			14. ___
15. ___			15. ___
16. ___			16. ___
17. ___			17. ___
18. ___			18. ___
19. ___			19. ___
20. ___			20. ___

MULTIPLE CHOICE UNIT TEST ANSWER KEY - *To Kill a Mockingbird*

Unit Test 1 answers are in the left column. Unit Test 2 answers are in the right column.

I. Matching	II. Multiple Choice	III. True or False	IV. Vocabulary
1. D L	1. A C	1. F F	1. D B
2. F N	2. D C	2. T F	2. A A
3. C K	3. D A	3. F T	3. C C
4. L T	4. C A	4. F F	4. C A
5. B J	5. B D	5. F F	5. D C
6. G O	6. A D	6. F F	6. A B
7. A I	7. C C	7. T T	7. C B
8. K S	8. B B	8. T F	8. D C
9. E M	9. C A	9. F F	9. C C
10. H P	10. A C	10. T T	10. B D
11. N B	11. D B		11. B A
12. I Q	12. C D		12. B B
13. J R	13. B A		13. D C
14. M A			14. C A
15. O C			15. B B
16. S G			16. C C
17. P D			17. A A
18. T H			18. C C
19. Q E			19. A D
20. R F			20. B B

UNIT RESOURCE MATERIALS

BULLETIN BOARD IDEAS - *To Kill A Mockingbird*

1. Save one corner of the board for the best of students' *Mockingbird* writing assignments.

2. Draw a map of Scout's neighborhood. Locate the Finch home, Miss Rachael's, Miss Maudie's, Miss Stephanie's, The Radley Place, Mrs. Dubose's, the school, the jail, and the courthouse.

3. Arrange the characters' names in cut-out letters on the board. Cut out pictures (or invite your students to find pictures) of people in magazines who look like each character. Post the best picture(s) near each name.

4. Take one of the word search puzzles from the extra activities packet and with a marker copy it over in a large size on the bulletin board. Write the clue words to find to one side. Invite students prior to and after class to find the words and circle them on the bulletin board.

5. Do a bulletin board about careers in law, law enforcement, and the justice system.

6. Do a bulletin board with information about youth crisis hotlines, etc. for kids like Dill who think no one at home cares and may be looking for somewhere to go.

7. Post articles about famous trials that have taken place (or trials that are currently taking place).

8. Divide your board into six sections--one section for each of the six themes that the groups discuss in Lesson Twelve. In the appropriate board sections, post articles and/or photos which illustrate each of the themes.

9. Write several of the most significant quotations from the book onto the board on brightly colored paper.

10. Do a bulletin board about the Civil Rights movement which attempted (attempts) to eliminate situations like Tom Robinson's.

11. As an alternate introductory activity, have students bring in things (pictures, drawings, anything that can be attached to your bulletin board) which represent ways in which they spend their summer vacation time. Have students post the items on the board and explain the significance of their items.

12. Make a bulletin board listing the vocabulary words for this unit. As you complete sections of the novel and discuss the vocabulary for each section, write the definitions on the bulletin board. (If your board is one students face frequently, it will help them learn the words.)

EXTRA IDEAS

One of the difficulties in teaching a novel is that all students don't read at the same speed. One student who likes to read may take the book home and finish it in a day or two. Sometimes a few students finish the in-class assignments early. The problem, then, is finding suitable extra activities for students.

The best thing I've found is to keep a little library in the classroom. For this unit on *To Kill A Mockingbird*, you might check out from the school library other related books and articles about the civil rights movement, how our justice system works, careers in the justice system, people's right to privacy, the crime of rape, mob violence, growing up and understanding the world, or accounts of trials that have taken place.

Other things you may keep on hand are puzzles. We have made some relating directly to *To Kill A Mockingbird* for you. Feel free to duplicate them.

Some students may like to draw. You might devise a contest or allow some extra-credit grade for students who draw characters or scenes from *To Kill A Mockingbird*. Note, too, that if the students do not want to keep their drawings you may pick up some extra bulletin board materials this way. If you have a contest and you supply the prize (a tape or something like that perhaps), you could, possibly, make the drawing itself a non-refundable entry fee.

The pages which follow contain games, puzzles and worksheets. The keys, when appropriate, immediately follow the puzzle or worksheet. There are two main groups of activities: one group for the unit; that is, generally relating to the *Mockingbird* text, and another group of activities related strictly to the *Mockingbird* vocabulary.

Directions for these games, puzzles and worksheets are self-explanatory. The object here is to provide you with extra materials you may use in any way you choose.

MORE ACTIVITIES - *To Kill A Mockingbird*

1. Pick a chapter or scene with a great deal of dialogue and have the students act it out on a stage. (Perhaps you could assign various scenes to different groups of students so more than one scene could be acted and more students could participate.)

2. Have students make a model of Maycomb or draw a map of the town. You could have them either stick only to the details given in the novel -- or you could let them create the details which are not given.

3. Show the film *To Kill A Mockingbird* after you have completed reading the novel in class. Have students evaluate the movie and compare/contrast it with the book. If the students have tried writing a chapter into a scene in a play, you may wish to discuss how the problems they encountered in changing the form were handled in the movie.

4. Have students design a book cover (front and back and inside flaps) for *To Kill A Mockingbird*.

5. Have students design a bulletin board (ready to be put up; not just sketched) for *To Kill A Mockingbird*.

6. Have students research and report on the status of civil rights in 1961, the year Harper Lee received the Pulitzer Prize for *To Kill A Mockingbird*.

7. Have students choose one chapter of the novel (with sufficient dialogue) to rewrite as a play. In conjunction with this assignment, have students write a composition explaining the difficulties they encountered in changing from one written form to another.

8. Hold a trial of your own in which the jury from *Mockingbird* is charged with the fictitious charge of "making an irresponsible decision." Have students work out who will prosecute, who will defend, who will be witnesses, and the entire scenario of the trial.

9. Have students write the script for one of the Boo Radley Games that Scout, Jem and Dill might have made up.

10. Have an attorney come to your classroom to discuss the judicial system, a specific trial, the duties of a lawyer, or just general questions students might have about what is and is not legal. If you could get the lawyer to agree to it, a discussion of Tom Robinson's trial from a "real" lawyer's point of view might be informative. (How he would have handled the case vs. how Atticus did, etc.)

WORD SEARCH - *To Kill A Mockingbird*

All words in this list are associated with *To Kill A Mockingbird*. The words are placed backwards, forward, diagonally, up and down. The included words are listed below the word search.

```
W C V Q F G D C R A W F O R D T C O O T I E S D
V E Y B L F I G T E Z E F B A L C O N Y R J R E
M N N N M V L L G C T A W Y R W C R S Y K E S Z
W A M I A O H A M K Q L L E B G D Q F Q M C E T
S E U L L P C J M E M O A E L O U N T M A M U M
J E H D N O M Y A R R E Y W A L O M U P T O H S
M A I X I O R O A K O R I T I S A S E N C C Y L
D R C N B E W A C M A N T C N H G K E S N D Z L
T S L K N Y Z D C N S I E I G T L M F I R E O B
K K F E T E U Q O I C C B N V A E I F N E Y M G
M N Y L E B P I D U H O I S I C C B N B K P M E
H A I Q O G S E S U R N X R L C C L O K A T F R
C U Y S E S I U R B N S T M O C K I N G B I R D
G S E E I K E C Z U T A J L Z Y R S E L N T C H
Z R B M L J H K C N T K Q D L E A A Z K I W D D
S C H O O L X C A E L U L A A I N R U P L A C Q
H E L E N B A P W C R I E D C T D E D I R P J M
```

ARM	DILL	KNIFE	READ
ATTICUS	DIRT	LAWYER	ROBINSON
AZALEAS	DOG	LEE	SCHOOL
BALCONY	DUBOSE	LINK	SCOUT
BOO	ESCAPE	LULA	SHOT
BRUISES	EWELL	MAUDIE	SUMMER
CAKES	FINCH	MAYCOMB	SYKES
CALPURNIA	FIRE	MAYELLA	TATE
CAROLINE	GILMER	MISSIONARY	TAYLOR
CECIL	GUILTY	MOB	TREE
CEMENT	GUM	MOCKINGBIRD	TRIAL
CHURCH	HAM	NORMAL	WALTER
COMPANY	HELEN	PAGEANT	YARD
COOTIES	INSIDE	PANTS	ZEEBO
CRAWFORD	JACK	PENNIES	
CRIED	JAIL	PRIDE	
CUNNINGHAM	JEM	RAYMOND	

CROSSWORD 1 - *To Kill A Mockingbird*

CROSSWORD CLUES *To Kill a Mockingbird*

ACROSS

2. Scout made a late entry and ruined it
8. It destroyed Miss Maudie's home
9. Atticus' occupation
11. Dolphus
13. It housed Tom Robinson while he waited for trial
14. Heck; the sheriff
16. Atticus' brother
17. To end the life of something
19. Atticus shot a mad one
22. Narrator
25. The Jacobs boy
26. Scout's pageant costume
28. A good time; having ---
30. They wanted to inflict their own justice on Tom
32. Mr. Deas; He escorted Helen
34. Bob or Mayella
35. Tom's left one was useless
36. Jem had to do it for Mrs. Dubose
37. Jem's got caught on the fence
39. Scout rubbed Walter's nose in it
40. Time of the year when Dill usually visited
41. To give assistance
42. Dill's initials
43. Also; a coordinating conjunction
44. Without companionship
45. Mayella's right side had lots of these
46. Cal's boy

DOWN

1. Preconceived idea
2. Mr. Cunningham had this; he would not take charity
3. Object found in the tree
4. Mr. Finch; Scout's dad
5. The hiding place for trinkets
6. Rev. at Cal's church
7. Object of the Radley games
8. Scout, Jem or Atticus
9. Woman at Cal's church who made Scout feel unwelcome
10. Boy Cunningham
12. Charles Baker Harris
15. Process by which innocence or guilt is determined
16. Scout's brother
17. Instrument that killed Bob Ewell
18. Author Harper
20. The prosecutor
21. -- *Kill A Mockingbird*
23. Miss Maudie made little ones for the children
24. The judge for Tom's trial
25. The Finch housekeeper, cook & nanny
27. Mrs. Merriweather's ----- circle
29. What Scout wanted Boo to be
31. Courage
33. Where Boo spent most of his time
37. Indian head ones were in the tree
38. Tom was shot while trying to -----
39. Jem chopped the tops off her camellia bushes
41. Mrs. Robinson

CROSSWORD ANSWER KEY - *To Kill A Mockingbird*

MATCHING QUIZ/WORKSHEET 1 - *To Kill A Mockingbird*

___ 1. Maycomb   A. What Burris Ewell had to go home and wash out

___ 2. Lawyer   B. Mrs. Merriweather's ----- circle

___ 3. Azaleas   C. Object of the Boo Radley game

___ 4. Background   D. Narrator

___ 5. Cooties   E. Time of year when Dill usually visited

___ 6. Alexandra   F. Miss Maudie's flowers

___ 7. Bruises   G. Where Boo spent most of his time

___ 8. Prejudice   H. Atticus' sister

___ 9. Inside   I. Indian head ones were in the tree

___ 10. Boo   J. Preconceived idea

___ 11. Missionary   K. Object found in the tree

___ 12. Gum   L. Scout and Jem went to Calpurnia's

___ 13. Scout   M. Miss Maudie made little ones for the children

___ 14. Shot   N. Name of the town and county

___ 15. Church   O. Cal's boy

___ 16. Pennies   P. Mayella's right side had lots of these

___ 17. Cunningham   Q. Walter

___ 18. Zeebo   R. The Cunninghams didn't have the proper --- to suit Alexandra

___ 19. Summer   S. Tom was --- trying to escape

___ 20. Cakes   T. Atticus' occupation

MATCHING QUIZ/WORKSHEET 2 - *To Kill A Mockingbird*

___ 1. Bravery   A. Miss Maudie made little ones for the children

___ 2. Guilty   B. Jem had to do it for Mrs. Dubose

___ 3. Azaleas   C. What Burris Ewell had to go home and wash out

___ 4. Background   D. Indian head ones were in the tree

___ 5. Pennies   E. Heck; the sheriff

___ 6. Ham   F. Tom's left was useless

___ 7. Lee   G. Courage

___ 8. Alexandra   H. Narrator

___ 9. Cooties   I. Scout, Jem or Atticus

___ 10. Inside   J. Atticus' brother

___ 11. Finch   K. Word to describe Miss Gates

___ 12. Hypocrite   L. The Cunninghams didn't have the proper --- to suit Alexandra

___ 13. Scout   M. Author Harper

___ 14. Escape   N. "He ain't ---, Cal, he's a Cunningham."

___ 15. Arm   O. Scout's pageant costume

___ 16. Cakes   P. The jury's verdict

___ 17. Tate   Q. Atticus' sister

___ 18. Read   R. Where Boo spent most of his time

___ 19. Jack   S. Miss Maudie's flowers

___ 20. Company   T. Tom was shot while trying to -----

KEY: MATCHING QUIZ/WORKSHEETS - *To Kill A Mockingbird*

Worksheet 1	Worksheet 2
1. N	1. G
2. T	2. P
3. F	3. S
4. R	4. L
5. A	5. D
6. H	6. O
7. P	7. M
8. J	8. Q
9. G	9. C
10. C	10. R
11. B	11. I
12. K	12. K
13. D	13. H
14. S	14. T
15. L	15. F
16. I	16. A
17. Q	17. E
18. O	18. B
19. E	19. J
20. M	20. N

JUGGLE LETTER REVIEW GAME CLUE SHEET - *Mockingbird*

SCRAMBLED	WORD	CLUE
DSEINI	INSIDE	Where Boo spent most of his time
IJLA	JAIL	It housed Tom Robinson while he waited for trial
SLAZAEA	AZALEAS	Miss Maudie's flowers
OGD	DOG	Atticus shot a mad one
MGU	GUM	Object found in the tree; chewing ---
AERBVRY	BRAVERY	Courage
NLKI	LINK	Mr. Deas; He escorted Helen
RMA	ARM	Tom's left one had been rendered useless
EDIUMA	MAUDIE	Neighbor who liked children and made cakes
NDRAMOY	RAYMOND	Dolphus
PLNCRAUAI	CALPURNIA	Finch housekeeper, cook and nanny
ITRLA	TRIAL	Process by which innocence or guilt is determined
SECKA	CAKES	Miss Maudie made little ones for the children
ESURMM	SUMMER	Time of year when Dill usually visited
SSEKY	SYKES	Rev. at Cal's church
IRTD	DIRT	Cal rubbed Walter's nose in it
YOABMCM	MAYCOMB	Name of the town and county
ILCEC	CECIL	The Jacobs boy
OOB	BOO	Arthur Radley
ADRE	READ	Jem had to do it for Mrs. Dubose
KMIRODNGCIB	MOCKINGBIRD	To Kill A ------
ULAL	LULA	Woman at Cal's church
IKFEN	KNIFE	Instrument that killed Bob Ewell
TATUSCI	ATTICUS	Mr. Finch; Scout's dad
ERIF	FIRE	It destroyed Miss Maudie's home
TRMOCOORU	COURTROOM	Where trials take place
ONONIBRS	ROBINSON	Tom or Helen
YTLIGU	GUILTY	The jury's verdict
UHNACGNMNI	CUNNINGHAM	Walter's last name
AMH	HAM	Scout's pageant costume
NIDTUAOCE	EDUCATION	What one gets at school
ACEESP	ESCAPE	Tom was shot while trying to ----
NDCEVEEI	EVIDENCE	Material proof
EFSRGUI	FIGURES	Two of these carved from soap were in the tree
AMNOYPC	COMPANY	"He ain't ---, Cal, he's a Cunningham."
AKJC	JACK	Atticus's brother
LELWE	EWELL	Bob or Mayella
EDRIP	PRIDE	Mr. Cunningham had this; would not take charity
OSTCEOI	COOTIES	What Burris Ewell had to go home and wash out
ENSIEPN	PENNIES	Indian head ones were in the tree

VOCABULARY RESOURCE MATERIALS

VOCABULARY WORD SEARCH - *Mockingbird*

All words in this list are associated with *To Kill A Mockingbird* with an emphasis on the vocabulary words chosen for study in the text. The words are placed backwards, forward, diagonally, up and down. The included words are listed below.

```
T N A D N E F E D D E R M I N G E N U O U S F K
U L D C T F J Z B S R N R X D G Q Y G N S M P N
E N A Z Q N L P Q S Q K C J L E B Y X C S A L L
H M A C Q U A I N T E D S U B T L E T Y U J I G
Y P E N I M I N F D X I D P M V L L G P T R T D
X H Q R I T D R G F S N R X E B E P E R E F T V
S D T A G M A T E I I U S A A R E R I P U Y Z T
M U B L J E O N M D L H B B R S S R U D S D M C
X L S V A E B U A R F A O S U O R E E C M I G G
Y D T T K E L Y S F D R M O E E P T V D S E D E
S W Y G A F T B V D P E I P L Q S M C E T B T B
P U R S U I T S I M T V B E E U U H E A R Y O Y
Q R C G T M N Q I D I D V A R N P E L T R E P F
A D J A C E N T R L U A S T T F S O N A N T S V
E V A S I O N T B A N A N W T I S I N T Z O X W
R X M J C B P O R T S E N H Y I N N V T W M C E
E L B I L L A F N I J Z V I S W Y G R E T N Q W
```

ACQUAINTED	ENCUMBERED	INGENUOUS	PERSEVERE
ACQUIRED	ENTRUSTED	IRKED	PURSUITS
ADJACENT	EVASION	IRRELEVANT	STEALTHY
AMIABLY	EXTRACT	ISOLATE	SUBSEQUENT
BEGRUDGE	FANATICAL	MALIGNANT	SUBTLETY
CONTEMPORARIES	FRAUD	OBLIVIOUS	SUSTAIN
DEBATING	IMPROBABLE	OBSCURE	TYRANNY
DEFENDANT	INAUDIBLE	PAUPER	UNANIMOUS
DISPELLED	INDULGE	PENSIVE	
EMERGE	INFALLIBLE	PERIL	

VOCABULARY CROSSWORD - *Mockingbird*

VOCABULARY CROSSWORD CLUES *To Kill a Mockingbird*

ACROSS
1. Supposedly; believed to be so but not yet proved
4. Poor person
7. Good-naturedly; cordially
9. -- *Kill A Mockingbird*
12. Object found in the tree
13. Activities; hobbies
15. Scout's pageant costume
16. Without sophistication; artless; innocent
18. Author Harper
20. The Jacobs boy
21. Mrs Robinson
23. Swayed back and forth in a seesaw motion
26. Finding out
29. Also; common coordinating conjunction
30. Tom's left one was useless
32. Danger
33. In complete agreement
35. Close to; next to
37. Dill's initials
38. The hiding place for trinkets
39. Time of year when Dill usually visited

DOWN
1. Passive agreement
2. To forcibly draw forth; pull out
3. To have done away with
5. Thoughtful
6. Inconspicuous; undistinguished; not well-known
8. To allow one a special pleasure
10. Troublesome situation
11. Atticus shot a mad one
14. Unavoidable; bound to happen
17. Departing from the established norm, model or rule
19. Annoyed; bothered
22. To go against
24. Extreme harshness; rigor
25. Obtained
27. To separate from the group; set apart
28. Deliberate deception for unfair or unlawful gain
31. Woman at Cal's church who made Scout feel unwelcome
34. They wanted to inflict their own justice on Tom
36. Scout's brother

VOCABULARY CROSSWORD ANSWER KEY - *Mockingbird*

	A	L	L	E	G	E	D	L	Y		P	A	U	P	E	R				O		
	C		X		I						E					A	M	I	A	B	L	Y
	Q		T	O	S	P					N	D				N	S					
G	U	M		R		P	U	R	S	U	I	T	S		O		D					
	I		H	A	M	E	E				N		I	N	G	E	N	U	O	U	S	
L	E	E		C		L	D		D	E	V		C		L		R					
	S		T		L	I		I		V	E		C		G		E					
		C		I	E		C	E	C	I	L		H	E	L	E	N		C			
T	E	E	T	E	R	E	D		A		T		A		N				O			
	N		Y		K			M		A	S	C	E	R	T	A	I	N	I	N	G	
	C		R	E	F			E		B	Q		R		S			T				
	E		A	N	D			R	N		L	U			I		O		A	R	M	
L			N		A	T		P	E	R	I	L		C	L		A		D	I		
U	N	A	N	I	M	O	U	S			R			A			D		I			
L		T	O	D		A	D	J	A	C	E	N	T		T		I		C			
A			C	B	H			E			D		T	R	E	E	C	T				
				S	U	M	M	E	R													

132

VOCABULARY WORKSHEET 1 - *Mockingbird*

___ 1. Teetered   A. Settlement of differences in which concessions are made

___ 2. Irrelevant   B. Oppressed; ill-treated and harassed

___ 3. Compensation   C. Not likely

___ 4. Fraud   D. To come forth from something

___ 5. Obscure   E. Native

___ 6. Unanimous   F. People who say they believe one thing but actually believe in the opposite

___ 7. Predicament   G. Extreme harshness; rigor

___ 8. Hypocrite   H. Deliberate deception for unfair or unlawful gain

___ 9. Indigenous   I. Authoritative statements

___ 10. Dispelled   J. Unaware

___ 11. Prejudice   K. Swayed back and forth with a seesaw motion

___ 12. Improbable   L. Things that cause trouble, lack of ease or difficulty

___ 13. Inconveniences   M. The condition of being puzzled

___ 14. Pronouncements   N. Not applicable; having nothing to do with the matter at hand

___ 15. Compromise   O. Preconceived preference or idea; bias

___ 16. Tyranny   P. Inconspicuous; undistinguished; not well-known

___ 17. Emerge   Q. To have done away with

___ 18. Persecuted   R. Troublesome situation

___ 19. Perplexity   S. In complete agreement

___ 20. Oblivious   T. Something given or received as substitution or payment

VOCABULARY WORKSHEET 2 - *Mockingbird*

___ 1. Pronouncements   A. Obtained

___ 2. Predicament   B. To keep in existence; maintain; prolong

___ 3. Ecclesiastical   C. Deliberate deception for unfair or unlawful gain

___ 4. Teetered   D. Without sophistication; artless; innocent

___ 5. Chameleon   E. Poor person

___ 6. Ingenuous   F. Authoritative statements

___ 7. Inaudible   G. Bring one's self down to an inferior level

___ 8. Dispelled   H. Unable to be heard

___ 9. Quibbling   I. To envy the possession or enjoyment of something

___ 10. Acquired   J. To have done away with

___ 11. Condescended   K. Act of avoiding

___ 12. Antagonize   L. In a self-satisfied manner

___ 13. Sustain   M. Incur the dislike of someone; counteract

___ 14. Adjacent   N. Pertaining to the church

___ 15. Unanimous   O. Close to; next to

___ 16. Pauper   P. Changeable person

___ 17. Fraud   Q. In complete agreement

___ 18. Evasion   R. Swayed back and forth in a seesaw motion

___ 19. Complacently   S. Making petty distinctions or irrelevant observations

___ 20. Begrudge   T. Troublesome situation

KEY: VOCABULARY WORKSHEETS - *Mockingbird*

Worksheet 1	Worksheet 2
1. K	1. F
2. N	2. T
3. T	3. N
4. H	4. R
5. P	5. P
6. S	6. D
7. R	7. H
8. F	8. J
9. E	9. S
10. Q	10. A
11. O	11. G
12. C	12. M
13. L	13. B
14. I	14. O
15. A	15. Q
16. G	16. E
17. D	17. C
18. B	18. K
19. M	19. L
20. J	20. I

VOCABULARY JUGGLE LETTER REVIEW GAME CLUES - *Mockingbird*

SCRAMBLED	WORD	CLUE
UGGDERBE	BEGRUDGE	To envy the possession or enjoyment of something
SOUECBR	OBSCURE	Inconspicuous; undistinguished; not well-known
ANTNRYY	TYRANNY	Extreme harshness; rigor
NYAMECCLTPLO	COMPLACENTLY	In a self-satisfied manner
IGALTNMAN	MALIGNANT	Actively evil in nature
AITDOCRCTN	CONTRADICT	To go against
ONPAHPRENEIS	APPREHENSION	Fearful feeling; dread
LOIUSVBOI	OBLIVIOUS	Unaware
CTEDEUPSER	PERSECUTED	Oppressed; ill-treated and harassed
RSDUNETTE	ENTRUSTED	Given over to another for care or protection
VLENAELTOM	MALEVOLENT	Having ill-will; malicious
ORABELIMPB	IMPROBABLE	Not likely
OETLADES	DESOLATE	Deserted
NLIEGUD	INDULGE	To allow one a special pleasure
KERDI	IRKED	Annoyed; bothered
STIUUPSR	PURSUITS	Activities; hobbies
REELIPYPXT	PERPLEXITY	The condition of being puzzled
MAUSUINON	UNANIMOUS	In complete agreement
RPLEI	PERIL	Danger
NOSUEGINU	INGENUOUS	Without sophistication; artless; innocent
BTELAEINIV	INEVITABLE	Unavoidable; bound to happen
EINAILUDB	INAUDIBLE	Unable to be heard
DNOECENST	CONSENTED	Agreed to
UEENUSTBSQ	SUBSEQUENT	Coming after
BAAILYM	AMIABLY	Good-naturedly; cordially
LOMEACNEH	CHAMELEON	Changeable; like the lizard which changes colors
GUIOSNINDE	INDIGENOUS	Native
ETETDVAMII	MEDITATIVE	Thoughtful; reflective
LBNIELILAF	INFALLIBLE	Unfailing; always correct
ONVASEI	EVASION	Act of avoiding
INACNSGTERAI	ASCERTAINING	Finding out
ECDATNAJ	ADJACENT	Next to
DMEECNREBU	ENCUMBERED	Hindered
AUFDR	FRAUD	Deliberate deception for unfair or unlawful gain
CECEIRTCN	ECCENTRIC	Departing from the established norm or model
EVPEREESR	PERSEVERE	Remain constant to a purpose in spite of obstacles
AIUNSST	SUSTAIN	To keep in existence; maintain; prolong

Mockingbird Vocabulary Clues Continued

TAECTRX	EXTRACT	To forcibly draw forth; pull out
NTCNEOEDS	CONSENTED	Agreed to
TNILRAREVE	IRRELEVANT	Not applicable; having nothing to do with the matter at hand
LTSOEAI	ISOLATE	To separate from the group; set apart
ERSMPOICMO	COMPROMISE	Settlement of differences in which concessions are made
ETESNMSASS	ASSESSMENT	Evaluation
MNARTEDPCIE	PREDICAMENT	Troublesome situation
ASNIUUMON	UNANIMOUS	In complete agreement
RUEAPP	PAUPER	Poor person
SELDPIELD	DISPELLED	To have done away with
IGBNQULIB	QUIBBLING	Making petty distinctions or irrelevant observations
CTSIREOPYH	HYPOCRITES	People who say they believe one thing but actually believe in the opposite
DQRAUECI	ACQUIRED	Obtained
IATLAFANC	FANATICAL	Possessed or driven by excessive zeal
UTSEBYLT	SUBTLETY	Something not obvious

www.ingramcontent.com/pod-product-compliance
Lightning Source LLC
Chambersburg PA
CBHW051415070526
44584CB00023B/3433